THE
WHITE HOUSE
AN HISTORIC GUIDE

50TH-ANNIVERSARY EDITION

D0731089

THE
WHITE HOUSE

AN HISTORIC GUIDE

50TH-ANNIVERSARY EDITION

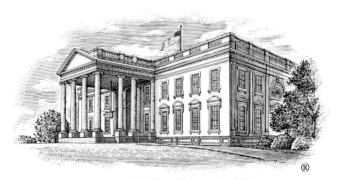

THE WHITE HOUSE
HISTORICAL ASSOCIATION

White House Historical Association
Washington, D.C.

The White House Historical Association is a nonprofit organization, chartered on November 3, 1961, to enhance understanding, appreciation, and enjoyment of the Executive Mansion. Income from the sale of this book will be used to publish other materials about the White House, as well as for the acquisition of historic furnishings and other objects for the Executive Mansion.
www.whitehousehistory.org

This book has been brought to publication through the generous assistance of the Hon. Walter H. Annenberg White House Publications Fund.

CONTENTS

vii - LETTER FROM FIRST LADY MICHELLE OBAMA

ix - PREFACE

x - ACKNOWLEDGMENTS

1 - INTRODUCTION

3 - THE WHITE HOUSE GROUNDS

41 - THE STATE FLOOR

107 - THE GROUND FLOOR

145 - THE SECOND FLOOR

193 - THE WEST AND EAST WINGS

229 - ILLUSTRATION CREDITS

231 - INDEX

THE WHITE HOUSE

August 6, 2010

Living at the White House is such an honor for our family, and every day, we feel the history that surrounds us. These are the halls of Lincoln and Roosevelt and the rooms of Jefferson and Eisenhower. The artistry of our greatest creators hangs on each wall and around every corner.

It is an impressive, inspiring place – but it is a home, too. It's that duality that makes the White House not just the President's residence, but truly the People's House. This house means something different for each of the thousands of people who visit each year. From students on school trips to families on vacation to church groups and senior citizens on organized tours, each memory is unique.

Since President Adams and his family first moved into the White House, it has grown and changed along with the country, all while maintaining its recognizable integrity. From bill signings to State Dinners to Easter Egg Rolls, this house serves as a backdrop to our national memory. Every day, a part of the American story unfolds here at the White House, just like it does at dinner tables and high school gyms and community centers all across this country.

In the following pages, you'll read more about the White House, its history, and its residents – and I hope when you're done, you'll feel a little bit more at home here, too.

Michelle Obama

The White House Historical Association has long been identified with its premier publication *The White House: An Historic Guide,* but it is with special pride that we present this Fiftieth-Anniversary Edition, the twenty-third edition in a sequence of revisions undertaken since the book was first published in 1962. Each edition has been enhanced by the contributions of first ladies, White House staff, and members of the association staff, but this edition brings together their work in a new way, guided by scholars and curators who have selected historic graphics, prints, engravings, and early photographs, as well as modern color photography, to show the house as it was and as it is today. What you see in these pages exemplifies the very extensive archive of historical documentation about the White House assembled over half a century by the White House Historical Association. We are especially pleased to open this edition with a letter from First Lady Michelle Obama, who thus continues the tradition of involvement in the guide that began with Jacqueline Kennedy.

This Fiftieth-Anniversary Edition also has a new purpose. In the twenty-first century considerations of heavy use of the White House for the business of the presidency, as well as its first purpose as a residence, combined with high-level security measures, have made the house less available for public tours than it was in the twentieth century. Therefore we planned this edition to allow the American people to get to know the White House even if they do not have an opportunity to visit. We hope it also exemplifies the spirit of the presidents and their families who have called the White House home yet always understood that it belongs to the American people.

Neil W. Horstman

PRESIDENT

WHITE HOUSE HISTORICAL ASSOCIATION

The White House Historical Association wishes to thank the many scholars, editors, writers, artists, photographers, and designers who over five decades have contributed to *The White House: An Historic Guide,* our flagship publication.

Betty C. Monkman, decorative arts scholar and former curator of the White House, oversaw the process of creating this Fiftieth-Anniversary Edition from concept to publication. She brought her unique firsthand knowledge of the White House collection, gained from more than thirty years of experience in the Office of the Curator and involvement with the guide through the production of many editions. William Seale, historian, wrote the architectural and historical text. He brings the story of the White House to life and makes it accessible for guests to the house and visitors to Washington, as well as to readers who never travel to the city.

The Office of the Curator has since the beginning written text, facilitated photography, and advised on necessary updates. With this edition Curator William G. Allman continued the tradition. Assistant Curator Lydia S. Tederick advised on the selection of historic photographs and coordinated the work of photographers commissioned by the association. The contributions of White House curators to the guide began with the first curator, Lorraine Pearce, who wrote the text for the first edition; subsequent editions were revised and enlarged by William V. Elder III, James R. Ketchum, Clement E. Conger, Rex W. Scouten, and Betty C. Monkman.

Ann Hofstra Grogg, consulting editor, meticulously shepherded the guide through each draft, creating a new and unique identity for this anniversary edition from the varied styles of our many contributors.

Many talented photographers have contributed to this book, and their body of work serves as a primary record of the decor and furnishings of the White House since 1962. Bruce White was the principal photographer for this edition. Several photographs by Peter Vitale taken during the George W. Bush administration are published here for the first time. White and Vitale join a long list that began with National Geographic photographers Bates W. Littlehales and George F. Mobley. We are pleased to remember the work of early photographers by opening many of the Second Floor chapters with a selection of their previously published room photographs. We also thank the White House staff members who accommodated our photographers and helped prepare for each shoot: Rear Admiral Stephen W. Rochon, Director of the Executive Residence and members of the Usher's Office; Dale F. Haney, Superintendant of the White House Grounds and the grounds crew; and the florists, engineers, and housekeepers.

We are pleased to present four new to-scale drawings created for this edition by the artist Rodica Prato. Her interior cutaway and exterior views reflect nearly two years of research and precise rendering of architectural details and current decor. The new look debuted with this edition was created by the talented designers at Pentagram.

Our special and personal thanks go to Robert L. Breeden, who oversaw the design and production of the first edition and served as editor through many editions during his tenure with the National Geographic Society. He continues to support and inspire us all as a member of the White House Historical Association board of directors.

THE
WHITE HOUSE

AN HISTORIC GUIDE

50TH-ANNIVERSARY EDITION

In 1962 President and Mrs. Kennedy were presented with the first two copies of *The White House: An Historic Guide,* upon its release. *Left to right:* President John F. Kennedy; David E. Finley, chairman of the Commission of Fine Arts; First Lady Jacqueline Kennedy; Melville Bell Grosvenor, president and editor of the National Geographic Society; Leonard Carmichael, secretary of the Smithsonian Institution; Melvin M. Payne, executive vice president and secretary of the National Geographic Society; Nash Castro, assistant superintendent, National Capital Parks Region of the National Park Service; Thomas Sutton Jett, regional director, National Capital Parks Region of the National Park Service; Lorraine Pearce, curator of the White House; and Robert L. Breeden, National Geographic Society.

In 1961, First Lady Jacqueline Kennedy resolved to make the White House a "living museum," and it was from her commitment to restoring the historic integrity of the mansion's public rooms that both the White House Historical Association and *The White House: An Historic Guide* came to be. Chartered to assist in acquiring and preserving works of art and historic furnishings for the White House, the association began sponsoring projects that interpret the historic White House to the American people. First among them was a guide to the White House, something that visitors could take with them as a memento to remind them, said Mrs. Kennedy, that "many First Families loved this house—and that each and every one left something of themselves behind in it." The National Geographic Society lent its staff and photographers to the project, and Mrs. Kennedy herself was the editor. The first edition of *The White House: An Historic Guide* was published in 1962, filled with color illustrations and room-by-room descriptions of decor and furnishings. Priced at just $1 at Mrs. Kennedy's insistence, the first edition of 250,000 copies sold out in ninety days. Work on a second edition began immediately.

Half a century later, this book remains the association's flagship publication. It has never been out of print. Updated and revised twenty-two times by first ladies and the association staff, it has now sold nearly 5 million copies. This twenty-third edition, a special Fiftieth-Anniversary Edition, is entirely new in plan, and entirely historic in content. It is designed for the visitor who may or may not have the opportunity to go inside the White House. A new section on the architecture and grounds allows study of the house from the street; new to-scale drawings allow an overview that a visitor in the house could never have; while traditional room-by-room descriptions allow everyone a "virtual visit," showcased through modern photography and enriched with historic images. The intent honors Mrs. Kennedy's commitment to making the human history of the White House available to all the American people.

THE
WHITE HOUSE
GROUNDS

THE PRESIDENT'S PARK

THE NORTH VIEW

THE SOUTH VIEW

THE
PRESIDENT'S PARK

The grounds surrounding the White House are for the use of the president and first family. They are usually open to the public a few times a year, on Saturday and Sunday afternoons in spring and fall, when the trees and flowers are at their peak seasons. There is no charge. The 18 acres of the White House grounds, within the iron fence, are the oldest continually maintained ornamental landscape in the United States. They are the result of two centuries of presidential interest and affection, especially for the noble old trees, whose number is continually replenished, so that the groves will never seem sparse or neglected when storm or age thins out the tree population.

The White House grounds or President's Park was originally 85 acres, the thought being that this "country house" would have its own orchards, pastures, cow barn, pigpens, chicken yards, and stables and be fairly well self-sufficient. Although Americans were a farming people in the 1790s, the work of a president even then was quite different from that of a farmer. So, while it was quickly realized that the White House was little suited to being a farm, early presidents were determined to farm nevertheless. John Adams, for example, ordered a vegetable garden planted in 1800, but was out of office and back home in Massachusetts before even the early peas were ready to harvest. Thomas Jefferson, believing the country house was better treated as a town house, fenced the grounds down to about 5 acres. Within that smaller area he and his nineteenth-century successors had both flower and vegetable gardens; fruit trees were popular, including one so cleverly grafted that it provided eight varieties of apple on one tree! In the 1850s the fences were extended to recover more of the original land. During Ulysses S. Grant's tenure they were moved even farther, and the great round fountains north and south, built on his orders, recall his interest in landscape.

The President's Park still exists as a legal entity, most of its 85 acres outside the iron fence and filled with streets and public buildings. Since the 1870s the White House grounds have totaled 18 acres, but the National Park Service has jurisdiction today over most of the original site established for it. Yet Lafayette Park, the Ellipse, the grounds of the Eisenhower Executive Office and Treasury Buildings, the grounds around some of the statuary and streets including Pennsylvania Avenue, East and West Executive Avenues, as well as the grounds immediately around the White House, are still identified as part of the historic President's Park set down by President George Washington.

It is noteworthy that George Washington himself situated the house on the ground upon which it stands. The city plan by Pierre Charles L'Enfant had the public buildings keyed to it, including this one, which was to be about five times the size it was when built. The smaller house designed by James Hoban in 1792 had to be placed in the much

The White House and President's Park are seen from above Lafayette Park, 2010.

larger space reserved. At a glance, the likely place to put the house was on the southeast side, in view from the Capitol, down Pennsylvania Avenue. Familiar with the plan of the city and ardently wanting it carried out, Washington decided otherwise, and instead personally drove stakes locating the house in the center of the north side of the site. In so doing he preserved the axis or line L'Enfant had designed in his city plan that ran north-south and crossed the east-west axis made by the Mall. L'Enfant wanted an equestrian statue of Washington to climax the intersection of the two axes; farther to the south L'Enfant intended that the axis be terminated by another monument, suggesting among other designs a pyramid. When the Washington Monument was begun in 1850, the swampy site caused it to be built a little eastward, apart from the intersection of the two axes. It was not until the Thomas Jefferson Memorial, built during the administration of Franklin D. Roosevelt, that the north-south axis was finally completed with a monumental termination.

THE
NORTH
VIEW

The following is meant to be used on the spot, taking advantage of views from outside the iron fence of the immediate grounds surrounding the White House

Begin the tour on Pennsylvania Avenue in front of the White House. The picture shows a typical White House day with visitors at the iron fence and workers repairing the house, oblivious to the clicks of dozens of cameras. Located inside the central entrance doorway facing Pennsylvania Avenue is the State Floor. It contains the public rooms of the White House—the East Room, Green Room, Blue Room, Red Room, State Dining Room, and other fine interiors pictured later in this guidebook. Private family quarters occupy the Second Floor, which appears as the "upstairs" from the street. The Third Floor cannot be identified from the street at all. Not counting subbasement work and storage areas, the White House is in fact a four-story house, within the historic two-story envelope of the original eighteenth-century structure. What one sees from Pennsylvania Avenue is the historic White House as known to almost all the American presidents.

On the north, the effect is, more or less, that of a front yard, with a liberal scattering of shade trees, lush grass, fountain, and driveway. James Monroe installed the stone gateposts in 1817; Andrew Jackson had them rolled on logs to their present position in 1833; the steel fencing and gates replicate the originals that were fashioned in wrought iron in 1817 by an Austrian American, Paulus Hedl, who lived in Westchester County, New York. Rutherford B. Hayes planted Ohio buckeyes along the driveway, interspersed with elms. Harry S. Truman planted the boxwoods in front of the North Portico when his remodeling of the White House was completed in 1952. In summer red salvia rings the fountain built by Ulysses S. Grant, and red geraniums abound in planters between the columns of the North Portico.

Apart from their distinguished history, the stone walls are remarkable specimens of early American stone construction, the work of two lodges of skilled stonemasons who sailed from Scotland for this project. The walls and carved details are superb. Note the richly ornamental "modillion" cornice, and, above the fan-shaped windows, the "blank" stone entablature that never received its intended carving.

The window surrounds display carved acanthus leaves (top) and Grecian chain or "guilloche" and "fish scale" brackets (middle). The State Floor windows (bottom) are surmounted by alternating arched and pedimented hoods. The great bulk of the house is reduced visually by these carvings and the later columned porticoes.

President Washington took special delight in fine stonework and enjoyed the dramatic effect of light and shadow upon both the smooth walls and intricate carvings. It is an effect enhanced by the traditional white paint. The climax of the fine stone masonry is the garlands of leaves, acorns, flowers, and fierce griffins that crown the main entrance. The draped festoon was hand-carved about 1795. Several forms of iron chisels were used to cut into the faces of two great stones, which, when finished, were hoisted with pulleys and rope to their present location and mortared together side by side, 14 feet across.

The Wings

The wings to the sides, east and west, were very early additions to the original house. Both were based upon drawings by President Jefferson and completed by his workmen in 1808. Congress, of course, paid all the bills. The wings were a means of organizing conveniently and out of sight the many functions then essential to a self-sufficient house—dairy, stable, laundry, smokehouse, root cellar, and so forth.

On the north, from Pennsylvania Avenue, the wings are barely visible, sunken closer to the lawn and showing only half-moon or lunette transoms for the admission of light into the interior. Today the wing on the east (on the left) houses the visitor's entrance, offices, and movie theater.

The original matching west wing (seen on the right of the house) contains the Press Room. Since 1902 the old wing has been connected to the Executive Office, or "West Wing," seen in the foreground.

This scene, from 1848, shows Lafayette Park, looking across Pennsylvania Avenue to the North Front.

There is bumper-to-bumper traffic on Pennsylvania Avenue, north side of the White House, on Sunday night, December 7, 1941, after the day's news of the attack on Pearl Harbor.

Pennsylvania Avenue was originally part of the White House grounds. James Monroe ordered the avenue cut through about 1822 and had by that time built an iron fence and the present stone gateposts. Lafayette Park was built about the same time and named for the Revolutionary War hero, the French general the Marquis de Lafayette, who made a triumphal return to America in 1824–25.

Before the avenue was extended here, the whole area, including Lafayette Park, served the community for market days. Even a horse race course rounded the area, and gambling was not omitted. It happened that on July 4, 1803, Thomas Jefferson stood at the north door of the White House and announced the Louisiana Purchase to hundreds of merrymakers. Departing unseen from the other side of the house, Meriwether Lewis, who had been Jefferson's secretary in the White House, headed for St. Louis to join George Rogers Clark for the famous expedition to the Pacific. So excited was the 29-year-old Lewis that he left his wallet behind.

Pennsylvania Avenue in front of the
White House, pictured in 2010, is now
a pedestrian street. It was closed to
traffic in 1995.

The Northwest Gate on Pennsylvania
Avenue is the main entrance for
business callers to the White House.
Flamboyant gas lamps were put atop the
original 1817 stone gate-piers in 1854.
The iron gates replicate the originals.

Throughout history, crowds have assembled before the White House for praise, curiosity, and sometimes for protest. In the nineteenth century when a president was in public favor, large numbers would march to the north yard at night and "call him out" to make a speech. Before amplification devices, no president was unfamiliar with "stump" speaking, which over the years had given political leaders finely developed voices with volume that made them heard clearly by big crowds.

From the front door on the North Portico presidents usually depart when their administrations are over (Richard M. Nixon, the only known exception, departed from the South Portico) and ride with the president-elect to the Capitol. The new president returns triumphant from his inauguration to enter the North Door. Heads of state, kings, and queens are received at this door by the president and first lady. Through the door and down the portico steps the coffins of deceased presidents are borne after lying in state in the East Room.

President Lincoln made his last speech from the window above the North Door of the White House.

Crowds gathered in front of the White House to view the funeral procession of President Franklin D. Roosevelt in April 1945.

In the past, movement to and from the front door was casual. Today's guards, enforcing strict security, smile when they hear stories of how easy it was in the 1920s and 1930s for people with convertibles to drive under the shelter of the North Portico to wait out a rainstorm. Such informality is no longer possible.

THE
SOUTH
VIEW

The best view from the south is from the sidewalk that runs along outside the south fence on E Street. There is always domestic activity on the south side. In this photograph, visitors watch as tree surgeons care for the Andrew Jackson Magnolias, damaged in a winter storm. From the "rear" or garden front, the White House does not seem as expansive as the setting that was created for it. George Washington originally approved a house about five times this size. City and site were laid out to serve the so-called palace. Cellars were dug; but Washington yielded to the same kind of economic pressures we know today and chose to build a more modest President's House. Plantings of all kinds, together with the enlarged East and West Wings, "stretch" the original house to make it seem in better scale for the broad ridge upon which it sits.

The White House grounds today within the fence feature an extensive grove of trees, with sloping lawns to the south and two formal gardens up near the house, the Rose Garden and the East Garden. The concept was devised in 1935 by Frederick Law Olmsted Jr., for Franklin D. Roosevelt.

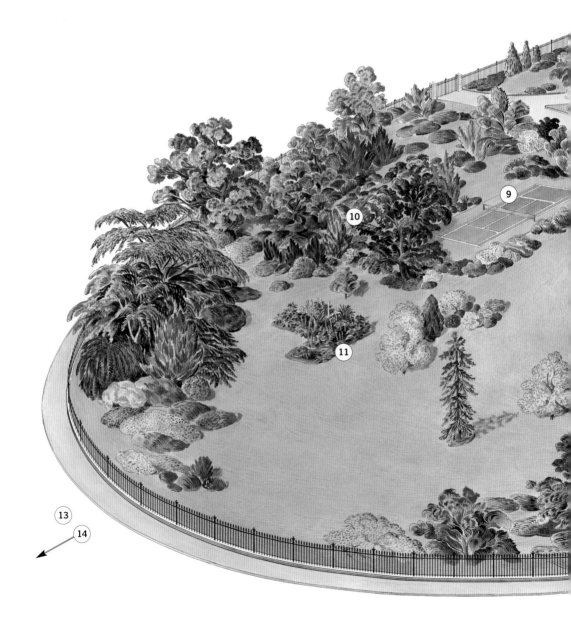

Architects of the White House

Three architects may be said to have built the White House. The first, who designed and erected it, was James Hoban, a native of County Kilkenny, Ireland. After British sailors burned the President's House on August 24, 1814, Hoban was engaged by the government to reconstruct it. At some point Hoban, perhaps working with drawings made by others, perhaps not, designed the building's two porches, that on the south in 1824 and the north 1829–30. He died in Washington in 1833, a man of substantial means and prominence. History remembers him as the man who built the White House.

The second most significant architect of the White House after Hoban was Charles Follen McKim, who renovated and rather "reinvented" the White House in 1902 for Theodore Roosevelt. Partner in the famous New York firm McKim, Mead & White, McKim was educated at Harvard College and at the École de Beaux-Arts in Paris, where students were schooled in melding modern building technology with historical design. His approach to Roosevelt's "restoration" of the White House would have pleased his Beaux-Arts masters.

The third, Lorenzo Simmons Winslow, was architect for Franklin D. Roosevelt and Harry S. Truman, both presidents with an interest in building and design. Winslow also studied at the École des Beaux-Arts, eventually taking employment with the National Park Service. He designed the White House swimming pool for President Roosevelt and stayed on to engage in many other White House projects. For President Truman he first built the Truman Balcony to the South Portico and then planned and supervised the entire renovation of the White House, 1948–52.

Other architects have worked on the White House in major ways. British-trained Benjamin Henry Latrobe built the east and west wings for Jefferson. The Philadelphian Thomas U. Walter, architect of the great Capitol dome, consulted on the White House with Millard Fillmore, Franklin Pierce, and Abraham Lincoln. The original Oval Office was designed in 1909 for President Taft by Washington architect Nathan C. Wyeth, while removal of the office to its present location was the work in 1934 of Eric Gugler of New York. From the mid-1920s until the late 1940s the famous Manhattan architect William Adams Delano gave sound advice, which helped preserve the White House inside and out from radical changes.

The main central block of the
house, the predominant part
of what one sees, with the south
projecting half-circle or bow
but not the columns, was
completed in 1798.

The south face of the house is
more decorative than the North
Front, being banded by tall vertical
wall-columns or pilasters, which
continue around the east and west
sides. Only the North Front does
not have pilasters.

The South Portico, with its double open-armed stairs, was completed in 1824 on order of President Monroe. With the exception of the slender second-level balcony built by President Truman in 1948, the portico is the only alteration to the south side of the house since 1824. The south wall itself is mostly original to the White House as built, having survived intact the British invasion and fire in 1814.

The south is the garden front of the White House, with rolling lawns and groves reserved for the first family's private use. The winding driveways are always pleasant for a walk, a jog, or a ride on a bicycle or golf cart. In the nineteenth century a bandstand was set up here, and one or two days a week the gates were open for Marine Band concerts and public promenades. Abraham Lincoln liked to lie on a sofa in the Blue Room, just behind the columns, shutters closed, and listen to the Marine Band unseen through the open window. Still held annually on the lawn is the Easter Egg Roll, which began as a local event at the Capitol, where children liked to roll their Easter eggs down the steep slope of Capitol Hill. In 1878, when the Capitol grounds were closed because the rolling disturbed the grass, Rutherford B. Hayes invited the children to come instead to his house. Today the event attracts thousands of children.

President Franklin D. Roosevelt gives his fourth inaugural address from the South Portico on January 20, 1945.

On the South Portico Franklin D. Roosevelt was inaugurated for his fourth term of office on January 20, 1945, three months before his death in April. The archway beneath the South Portico is where the family usually enters the house. Once inside they take the elevator upstairs to the family quarters. Through the arch diplomats and special guests call at the White House and are received in the Diplomatic Reception Room just inside the door. On the broad lawn the president's helicopter is likely to land any time of any day, taking or returning him from some appointment or from Andrews Air Force Base in Maryland, where *Air Force One* always awaits, ready to go anywhere the president may need to go in the world.

When a foreign head of state visits the president, this individual is received officially on the South Lawn, with the South Front of the White House as a dramatic backdrop. When the guest arrives from Blair House (across Pennsylvania Avenue) in an official car, the president and first lady walk out to extend their welcome. The Marine

Looking directly toward the front door of the house from the Pennsylvania Avenue sidewalk, imagine the central or main block of the house without the North Portico: it would look as it did when construction was finished about 1798, as shown in this detail from an original elevation, 1793.

The North Portico (or porch) with its three-sided colonnade of stone was added in 1829–30, thirty years after the White House was completed.

Originally the White House was a two-story structure with a basement, as this 1806 watercolor by the architect Benjamin Henry Latrobe suggests. On the north the basement was concealed by the site's higher grade, so the house appears to be just two stories set squarely on the ground. Looking from the south, the basement is visible as the Ground Floor.

PENNSYLVANIA AVENUE

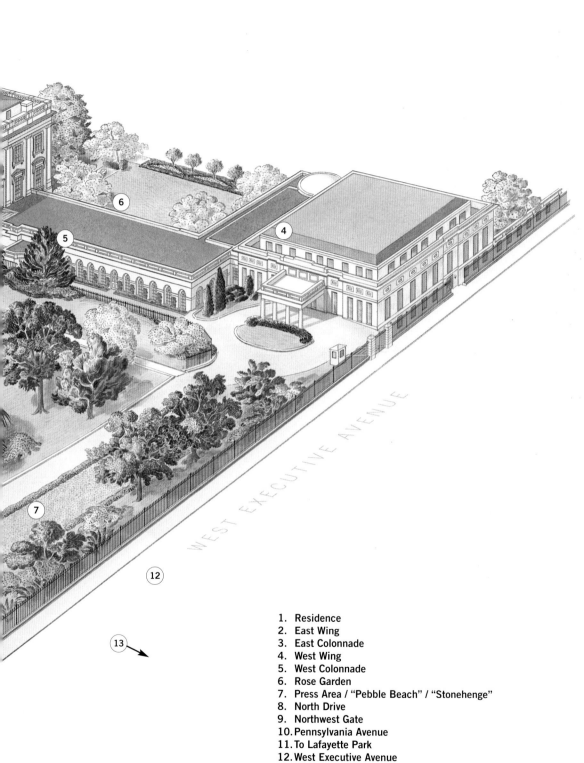

1. Residence
2. East Wing
3. East Colonnade
4. West Wing
5. West Colonnade
6. Rose Garden
7. Press Area / "Pebble Beach" / "Stonehenge"
8. North Drive
9. Northwest Gate
10. Pennsylvania Avenue
11. To Lafayette Park
12. West Executive Avenue
13. To the Eisenhower Executive Office Buildling
14. East Executive Avenue
15. To the Treasury Building

1792: What Sort of House Suits a President?

George Washington built for the presidency an ambitious house (if not the palace one might have expected he would want) that might match the vast constitutional powers of his office. On his own request he met with the Charleston, South Carolina, builder James Hoban and set upon a design for the President's House probably suggested by Hoban. Thomas Jefferson feared the president might build a house to the scale of the Federal City plan that Washington had approved and that Jefferson found overblown and princely. To ward off the decisions he feared, Jefferson proposed an advertised competition: may the best plan win. Washington agreed to this, perhaps with more patience than enthusiasm.

The competition was duly advertised. Many plans were sent in, including an anonymous entry that, if not by Jefferson, was certainly made under his supervision. Most submitted plans that we know about show a broad range of ideas regarding the image the president might project through his house. It was a job recently created in the Constitution, and its trappings were subject to discussion. Architects, builders, and poets exercised their imaginations: several entries resembled enlarged courthouses, others churches, and still others small palaces. Among the plans that survive, all of them have at least one very large room, and in one plan the large room housed a throne. Hoban's entry was entirely different from the others, seeming more a house than a public building. This was what Washington wanted. He duly reviewed the entries in mid-summer 1792 and selected Hoban's, which proposed a handsome, though by British standards modest, English or Irish type of country house. With modifications, this was the White House we know today.

CONSTRUCTION TIMELINE
OF THE WHITE HOUSE

* July 1792, President George Washington approves the design and plans of James Hoban for the "President's House."

* October 13, 1792, cornerstone set in the mortar of a completed stone foundation wall.

* November 1798, structure of the White House is completed, and the sand-colored stone walls are whitewashed.

* 1805–8, President Thomas Jefferson builds the first east and west wings.

* August 24, 1814, invading British sailors burn the White House to its stone walls. It is one of the dramatic events in the War of 1812.

* Winter 1814, decision is made to rebuild the White House as it was.

* January 1, 1818, President James Monroe opens the reconstructed White House at a gala New Year's reception.

* 1824, South Portico is constructed by Hoban; it looks toward the Potomac River.

* 1829–30, North Portico is constructed by Hoban; it faces Pennsylvania Avenue.

* 1866, Jefferson's east wing is demolished and replaced with small porch.

* 1902, White House is "restored" and updated by President Theodore Roosevelt, establishing a pattern of use still followed today; first West Wing office is built, attached to the originial 1808 west wing or West Colonnade.

1. Entrance Hall
2. East Room
3. Green Room
4. Blue Room
5. Red Room
6. State Dining Room
7. Family Dining Room
8. Cross Hall
9. Grand Staircase

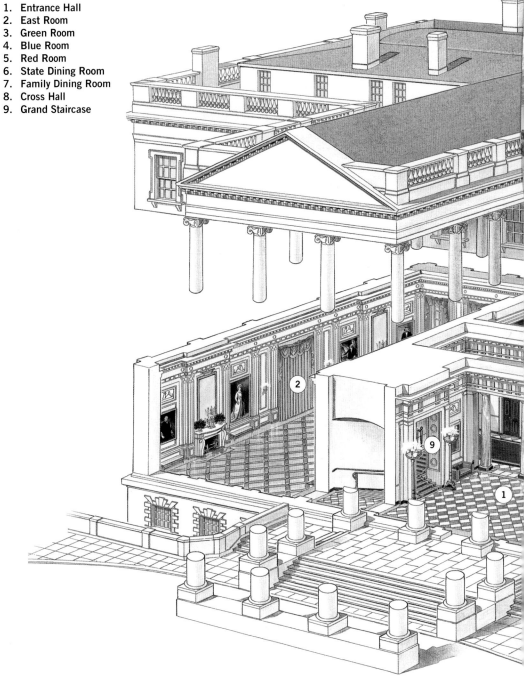

Band stands on the double stairs and on the porch, and bleachers are provided for special guests and the press. Hundreds of guests stand on the lawn. United States military servicemen fall in formation. President and dignitary shake hands, review the troops on foot, and, standing on a platform together, make brief remarks. They depart to the house or through the Rose Garden to the Oval Office. It is a short ceremony, about 30 minutes, appropriate to the occasion while costing the busy president and his official guest very little work time.

The West Wing is connected to the White House by Jefferson's 1808 West Colonnade, which has been wrapped around the 1902 wing to provide shade to its important rooms, including the Oval Office and Cabinet Room.

Queen Elizabeth II, beside President George W. Bush, speaks from a podium on the South Lawn during the arrival ceremony for her official visit in May 2007.

The Ground Floor on the north falls below the level of the lawn and is entirely invisible from the street. Light to its rooms is provided by a deep areaway, rather like a "dry moat." The temporary awning in this photograph shelters from unpredictable weather flower arrangements headed for the State Dining Room upstairs.

Originally there was an attic beneath the roof, lighted by dormer windows and concealed from view by the stone balustrade crowning the stone walls. It contained bedrooms for servants, but the attic's great height was believed unsafe and in the early days it was used only for storage. Today's Third Floor replaced the attic in 1927.

The Finest Stonework in Eighteenth-Century America

The dressed or smooth stones that make up the walls, columns, and all other elements but the doors and window sashes, which are wood, were quarried down the Potomac River in a sandstone outcropping on Aquia Creek in Stafford County, Virginia. Relative to limestone, sandstone is a soft material, quite porous. Removed from the quarry to this site, it was sawed into blocks and either smoothed and shaped for the walls or carved into ornaments. Each area of stone was first laid out complete on the ground, numbered, and once approved as perfect, taken up to the walls by a wooden crane, set in place, and secured with mortar. This modern photograph shows a window "hood" stripped of paint and revealing scorch marks from the burning of the house in 1814.

Once the stone walls were completed, they were coated with a tough lime-based "whitewash" that filled the many holes and crevices natural to the stone, thus rejecting rainwater, which, should it freeze in severe winter weather, would expand and might crack the stone. The house was restored after the British invasion in 1814, parts of the walls rebuilt exactly as they had been. Because the builders reused stone that was still solid, the reconstructed walls were such a patchwork and scarred with soot that they were covered with oil paint. But the presidential residence had already been called "The White House" for at least a decade, thanks to the original whitewash. Here painters apply the first coat of fresh white paint after the twenty-year cleaning and conservation of the stone, commenced in 1980.

1. Entrance Hall
2. East Room
3. Green Room
4. Blue Room
5. Red Room
6. State Dining Room
7. Family Dining Room
8. Library
9. Vermeil Room
10. China Room
11. Diplomatic Reception Room
12. Map Room

CONSTRUCTION TIMELINE
OF THE WHITE HOUSE

* 1909, West Wing is doubled in size by President William Howard Taft, to include the Oval Office, the oval shape inspired by the Blue Room.

* 1927, Roof and attic are replaced by President Calvin Coolidge with a new roof of steeper pitch, to accommodate a new Third Floor within, where a smaller attic had been.

* Christmas Eve 1929, West Wing is gutted by fire.

* 1930, President Herbert Hoover lays aside his extensive plans for remodeling the West Wing and, because of the Depression, orders its reconstruction much as it was.

* 1934, President Franklin D. Roosevelt triples the size of the West Wing, moves the Oval Office adjacent to the Rose Garden.

* 1942, East Wing is expanded with addition of a two-story structure.

* 1947–48, President Harry S. Truman builds a second-story balcony to the South Portico

* 1948–52, Truman supervises the complete reconstruction of the White House within the historic stone shell. The house of 64 rooms becomes one of 132 rooms.

* 1970, President Richard M. Nixon adds a columned porch to the front of the West Wing, patterning the design on Jefferson's architectural design of the adjacent West Colonnade.

* 1980, President Jimmy Carter orders the cleaning and conservation of the paint-scaled stone walls; the process continues for nearly twenty years, being finally completed during the administration of President Bill Clinton. The house is repainted the warm white that in the twentieth century had replaced the stark white of the early years.

THE
STATE FLOOR

THE ENTRANCE HALL

THE CROSS HALL

THE GRAND STAIRCASE

THE EAST ROOM

THE GREEN ROOM

THE BLUE ROOM

THE RED ROOM

THE STATE DINING ROOM

THE FAMILY DINING ROOM

THE
ENTRANCE
HALL

The imposing Entrance Hall receives the visitor inside the White House. Straight ahead in this view from the North Portico are the emblems of office at the door of the Blue Room—the Presidential Seal, the presidential flag, and the flag of the United States. The tiled floor is Tennessee marble, while the richly striated columns are Georgia marble. Between the central columns, brass stars inset on the floor mark the location of time capsules that commemorate the 1902 and 1948–52 renovations of the house. The play of light on hard surfaces lends an austerity to the Entrance Hall that reinforces its official formality.

Built to serve crowds, the Entrance Hall has looked more or less the same since the house was built. Different columns and marble floors instead of early-day wood or colored tiles mark changes. Martin Van Buren installed window glass between the columns in 1837 to block drafts; Chester A. Arthur in 1882 commissioned the designer Louis Comfort Tiffany to replace the glass with colored glass, thus the famous "Tiffany screen." Otherwise the early presidents would recognize the hall today.

Through all this time, the Entrance Hall has always been what its name implies. Guests of state enter here for formal State Dinners, the president and first lady greeting them on the steps outside. The United States Marine Band is situated in the hall on the west side. When at a state affair the president enters, he and his party descend the Grand Staircase and the Marine Band plays "Hail to the Chief." The president and main guests pause on the landing for a photograph, then proceed to join the greater number of people already assembled.

Thomas Jefferson served banquets in the Entrance Hall and developed a museum of artifacts brought from the newly acquired Louisiana Territory by explorers Meriwether Lewis and William Clark (1803–6) and Zebulon Pike (1805–7). The curiosities included Indian costumes and pottery, specimen plants, and even a pair of live bear cubs, for which the animal-loving Jefferson built a pen just outside the front steps.

In the nineteenth century, almost everyone who came to the White House arrived on the State Floor through the North Door into the Entrance Hall. During large social events, coats and umbrellas were stashed here. Since Theodore Roosevelt's renovation of 1902, most people

The Entrance Hall (illustrated here in a late nineteenth-century newspaper) in early days was as busy as a hotel lobby, with all callers stopping to be dispatched either upstairs to the president's office, to visit with the first family, or to tour the State Rooms.

have entered though the East Wing, ascending from the Ground Floor to the State Floor and converging in the Entrance Hall. The space is sometimes used for receiving lines and for dancing. It also continues its earlier purpose as a "bandstand" for the Marine Band, which first played here in 1801 for Thomas Jefferson. Although maintained for its historic function on special occasions, the Entrance Hall today is for most White House visitors an exit rather than an entrance, for the usual entrance has been located in the East Wing for more than a century.

Victorian efforts to make the hall seem less like a cold public place resulted in the refinements of Aesthetic decoration, climaxed by Louis Comfort Tiffany's colored glass screen, which was the wonder of all who saw it, including this group of admiring visitors in 1889 during the administration of President Benjamin Harrison.

The Marine Band, seen here in 2000 resplendent in red dress jackets, often performs in the Entrance Hall for White House official events. Known as "The President's Own," the Marine Band has many component talents, from the brass band, to strings to jazz. Its musicians are career members of the United States armed forces, with White House music as their gig.

The Usher's Room shown here in 2008 is located just off of the Entrance Hall. As the principal executive for the management of the residence, the chief usher is responsible for any expenditures of federal money involving the White House.

FINE AND DECORATIVE ARTS

Portraits of recent presidents have traditionally hung in the Entrance Hall, the only works of art in this sparsely furnished space. The hall is lighted by a handsome English cut-glass chandelier, c. 1775, and gilded bronze light standards from the Theodore Roosevelt renovation of 1902.

On the carved and gilded pier table from the Oval Room suite purchased by President Monroe is a gilded bronze clock with the figure of Minerva, the Roman goddess of wisdom. Both were made in Paris, c. 1817.

THE
CROSS
HALL

This lofty corridor, running east to west, unites the State Rooms of the White House, with the East Room and State Dining Room at opposite ends and the Red, Blue, and Green Rooms opening from the right or south side. Through the row of columns on the north side is the Entrance Hall. The slightly arched ceiling springs from a deep cornice made of cast plaster, designed for the Theodore Roosevelt renovation of 1902. The lectern set on a platform in the distant East Room indicates that a presidential address or news conference will soon take place. Although primarily a passage, where guests walk to dinner and receptions down its elegant span, the Cross Hall is also a gallery of portraits of recent presidents.

The present architecture of the Cross Hall, completed in 1952 by the White House architect Lorenzo S. Winslow, combines the original neoclassical idea of the eighteenth-century house with the monumentality introduced by the architects McKim, Mead & White in 1902. The original columns were carved from the bluish marble quarried in King of Prussia, Pennsylvania; those in place now are the fourth set to grace the hall since 1800. Stone floors that George Washington envisioned for the hall were not realized until 1902 with the introduction of Joliet stone paving; in 1952 Harry S. Truman approved marble, and the earlier stone flooring went to a landfill. Beneath the floor, between the central columns, are the twentieth-century time capsules of the White House, first put there in 1902, then revised and reinstalled in 1952.

A dinner given by President McKinley for the diplomatic corps in Washington was set in the Cross Hall, about 1900.

Old newspapers, handwritten notes from workmen, and a whiskey bottle were among the treasures revealed when the first time capsule was eagerly opened in 1950.

The presidential portraits displayed here are traditionally of those most recently in office. But the "rule" is that there is no rule about it, for the house is the president's home for the duration of his administration and he may adorn the hall as he wishes.

In the late nineteenth century, when the Tiffany screen extended between the columns, the Cross Hall was used sometimes as a spillover dining room, light passing through the colored glass making splashes of red, white, and blue over the white damask tablecloth and napkins. The two niches have always been here. For James Madison they held iron heating stoves concealed in classical-style urns made of cement. In 1902, when the State Dining Room was expanded, the Grand Staircase was relocated from its original space at the west end of the Cross Hall to a new site adjacent to the East Room.

At the conclusion of musical evenings today the guests move from the East Room to the Entrance and Cross Halls for refreshments and to dance to the music of the

Marine Band. The president and first lady are likely to bid their guests good night at this point and walk to the elevator, while the company may remain for a while longer. In leaving the guests descend to the Ground Floor to retrieve their coats and depart through the East Wing.

Above: This view of the Cross Hall, looking toward the East Room, is from the Hayes administration, c. 1880.

Right: Following his final address to the nation as president, President George W. Bush departs alone from the East Room down the Cross Hall toward the doors of the State Dining Room, January 15, 2009.

THE
GRAND
STAIRCASE

Entirely filling the alcove that contains it, the Grand Staircase is the formal connection between the family quarters and the State Floor. On official occasions the president descends this stair, to the Marine Band's rousing "Hail to the Chief." Presidents have taken great interest in the grand staircases because of the entrance ceremony, but none to the extent of Harry S. Truman. He found the official entrance awkward using the previous staircase, and when he rebuilt the interior of the White House in 1948–52 revised it to the gentle descent in two ranges of steps, down to the stagelike landing or platform, where he would first appear before his guests.

THE GRAND STAIRCASE
ARCHITECTURE AND HISTORY

The current Grand Staircase is the fifth in the White House. Thomas Jefferson built the first, in the west end of the Cross Hall, an area now incorporated into the north end of the State Dining Room. This was replaced when the house was rebuilt in 1817 and replaced and redesigned in 1869. The last two were in the present location off the Entrance Hall, in the renovations by Theodore Roosevelt in 1902 and by Harry Truman, finished in 1952.

A grand staircase on its least significant level provides ascent to the next floor up; but that function is also served at the White House by other staircases and an elevator. The main role of such a stair, and why it is grand, is because it enhances and dramatizes the descent of people into a room. On this grand stair the principal figures begin a state occasion by presenting themselves to the other guests, who have already arrived. Presidential entrances have always been carefully planned. Andrew Jackson's, for example, were made direct from the Cross Hall into the East Room, where all the guests were already assembled: wearing a high-collared blue cape over his frail frame, Jackson passed through the arched doorway, over which a galaxy of gilt stars had been pasted to the wallpaper to frame him in heroic splendor.

The main role of the Grand Staircase of the White House is still for formal entrances. Otherwise, seldom used, it rises to locked doors. "Arrival ceremonies," as the entrances are called, present exciting moments, with the Marine Band playing a vigorous "Hail to the Chief," the crowd of guests stretching to see as the principal figures descend to the music, photographers poised to snap, and the president, first lady, and their party arriving at the landing, facing the

The platform landing of today's Grand Staircase was designed under the very precise direction of President Truman to accommodate picture-taking, and it was put to good use here. In this 1961 photograph, President and Mrs. Kennedy have invited the Truman family to return to the White House for dinner. President and Mrs. Truman stand on the left, with the Kennedys on the right, and in the rear are Margaret Truman Daniels and Clifton Daniels, flanked by White House social aides.

Entrance Hall, where they pause to be seen by all before proceeding to the East Room or Blue Room to form a receiving line.

Entering a State Dinner from the Grand Staircase, President and Mrs. Obama pose with Felipe Calderón, president of the Mexican Republic, and his wife Margarita Zavala, May 19, 2010.

THE
EAST ROOM

The great ceremonial room of the White House, the East Room is an elegant space, richly finished and sparsely furnished. The largest room in the house and extending the full length of the building, north to south, it is 85 feet long and 40 feet wide. The decor retains the international flair introduced in 1902 by Theodore Roosevelt, whose portrait hangs in the southeast corner. Always painted white, the ornate walls and ceiling borrow from eighteenth-century French and English design. The chandeliers, light standards, benches, and window cornices remain from the 1902 renovation. Usually empty, the East Room awaits whatever temporary furniture might be needed—chairs, platforms, musical instruments—to serve the wide variety of heavily attended events held constantly during a president's term.

The East Room was designed for crowds, and presidential receptions are no exception. This one, held by President Buchanan in 1858, was published in *Harper's Weekly* and shows the room in its pre–Civil War splendor. Uniforms of the diplomats spangle the throng, while women's voluminous skirts, low, lace-framed necklines, and oiled hair make a fashion statement for the era, all reflected in broad mirrors and lighted by glass chandeliers.

After being an unfinished, barren, brick-walled interior for the first nearly thirty years, the East Room was completed in 1829 for Andrew Jackson. By this time the once-casual name had stuck. Jackson decorated the grand space in yellow and royal blue and installed the first triple-matched glass chandeliers. Those in place today are only the third set to hang in the room. Jackson's originals were replaced in 1873 by Ulysses S. Grant's glass "gasoliers," and the present electric fixtures of gilt bronze and cut glass were hung there by Theodore Roosevelt in 1902. Harry S. Truman installed the red marble mantels in 1952.

Central to the gallery of portraits that today line the east wall is Gilbert Stuart's of George Washington, purchased by Congress on July 5, 1800, and installed in the White House by November 1, 1800, when John Adams moved in. This is the same picture that First Lady Dolley Madison sent to last-minute safety on August 24, 1814, just before she fled from the muskets and cannon of invading British troops marching on Washington during the War of 1812. The companion portrait of First Lady Martha Washington was commissioned by Rutherford B. Hayes in 1878 from E. F. Andrews, who borrowed the head from Gilbert Stuart's life portrait of Mrs. Washington in later life and the body from the president's lithe 20-year-old niece, Emily Platt.

President Washington intended this grand space as an "audience room," where the president would receive Congress en masse, to present bills for his consideration. Such princely events were staged by the "Federalist" government of the Founding Fathers to dramatize the power of leadership; Thomas Jefferson, the "Republican" successor, trimmed away ceremony to show that power lay with the people. Rendered obsolete by the new Jeffersonian idea, this greatest of the State Rooms had its barnlike vastness partitioned as living quarters for Meriwether Lewis, the president's secretary, prior to the Lewis and Clark expedition to the West.

The most auspicious events attached to the East Room in the first 125 years of the White House were the public receptions. There were originally two, New Year's Day and the Fourth of July, when the president received the diplomatic corps and the general public. No invitations were required, and thousands attended. July 4 was not celebrated after 1876, but the New Year's event continued until 1932.

Used today for every sort of function from televised addresses to press conferences to after-dinner musical programs, the East Room provides an elegant setting for whatever purpose the president may desire. Political and diplomatic events bring the room closest to its original

President Lincoln's body lay in state in the center of the East Room, and thousands of mourners passed by. The awning and bier were built for the funeral, and the bier was retained and has been used at every presidential funeral since 1865. For the Lincoln funeral more than a thousand invited guests crowded low bleachers around the walls, suffering nearly unbearable heat and the heavy fragrance of spring flowers. The newspaper artist, Alfred Waud, who made his sketch in advance, drew Mrs. Lincoln standing at the coffin's head, naturally assuming she would be there, but she stayed upstairs in bed, too grief stricken to attend.

President Hayes sits in the elaborately Victorian East Room, 1881, meeting with a delegation of Plains Indians, accompanied by their government agent. Such intimate conversations with Native Americans, sponsored by the federal government, were traditional in the White House from President Jefferson's time through the end of America's frontier period, about 1890.

intent. In May 1908 for the first Conservation Conference, Theodore Roosevelt assembled 360 men and women here, representing government and private interests, all activists who envisioned America's future public lands and parks. Lyndon B. Johnson signed the Civil Rights Act here on July 2, 1964. On September 17, 1978, Jimmy Carter brought Anwar al-Sadat, president of Egypt, and Menahem Begin, prime minister of Israel, together in the East Room to sign the Camp David Accords. Cabinet members, Supreme Court justices, and many other officials take their oaths of office in the East Room.

Notable weddings that have taken place in the East Room include those of Nellie Grant, Ulysses S. Grant's daughter, in 1874; Theodore Roosevelt's daughter Alice in 1906; and Lyndon B. Johnson's daughter Lynda in 1967, which was attended by the widowed 83-year-old Alice Roosevelt Longworth.

In Theodore Roosevelt's 1902 remodeling of the White House, Victorian embellishments of plaster were buried beneath reproduction "historical" French-style wood paneling. The international look of the new East Room decor, climaxed by giant electric chandeliers of glass, reflected a new image of America as a world power. The same fixtures remain in place today.

The East Room, July 2, 1964, was the setting for President Johnson's signing of the Civil Rights Act. Dr. Martin Luther King Jr. looks on proudly.

Seven presidents have lain in state in the East Room, their flag-draped coffins beneath the central chandelier—William Henry Harrison (1841), Zachary Taylor (1850), Abraham Lincoln (1865), William McKinley (1901), Warren G. Harding (1923), Franklin D. Roosevelt (1945), and John F. Kennedy (1963). At these sad times the chandeliers and mirrors are draped in black crape.

Chandeliers, bronze light standards, carved and gilded benches and window cornices, and bronze andirons, all in revival styles popular in the early twentieth century, were commissioned for the East Room during the Theodore Roosevelt changes of 1902 and remain in place today.

Opposite: Congress purchased this 1797 portrait of George Washington by Gilbert Stuart in 1800, the first work of art acquired for the new President's House. This iconic image survived the fire of 1814 due to the thoughtful action of First Lady Dolley Madison.

One of a pair of gilded bronze French candelabrum with military trophies in relief on the base, this was placed in the Oval Room of James Monroe in 1817. The pair reside on an East Room mantel today.

Theodore Roosevelt commissioned John Singer Sargent to paint his official portrait in the White House. It was completed in 1903. Posed on a White House staircase, the portrait pleased Roosevelt, who later wrote that he liked it "enormously."

THE
GREEN
ROOM

The Green Room, the first of the State Rooms to be named for the color of its textiles, is furnished in the late Federal style popular when the White House was first occupied. The furniture is not original to the room but was acquired in the 1970s. The silk wall fabric, initially selected by First Lady Jacqueline Kennedy in 1962, has been replaced several times, most recently by First Lady Laura Bush in 2007. Draperies of a period design and a reproduction French rug complement an Italian marble mantelpiece. Paintings include portraits of presidents and significant works by American artists. The least formal of the state parlors, the Green Room provides a serene setting for small gatherings, interviews, teas, and social activities.

THE GREEN ROOM
ARCHITECTURE AND HISTORY

The state parlors are more domestic in scale than the grand Entrance Hall or East Room, and among them the Green Room has a particularly inviting quality that welcomes callers and guests. But the Green Room's first use may have been as a bedchamber for John Adams's secretary. If so, it was soon reconfigured as a dining room by Adams's successor, Thomas Jefferson, who covered the board floor with washable green-painted canvas and installed a round table at the center and on its corners small "dumb waiters" (furniture for food service that, unlike human waiters, could not hear and tell). President Jefferson entertained carefully crafted lists of politicians, disguising his political motives in food and wine, which from all accounts were excellent. Among the many notables with whom he dined in this room were the poet Joel Barlow; Thomas Paine, the publicist patriot whose book *Common Sense* had helped stir the coals of revolution in America and France; and in 1805 the South American revolutionary Francisco de Miranda.

The Green Room in the early nineteenth century was more isolated from the other State Rooms than today by having fewer doors into it. This proved a convenience for that consummate politician James Madison, who at White House entertainments cornered visiting politicians here, to make his points. The green decorative scheme adopted by his successor, James Monroe, must have been striking, for Monroe's successors retained the color in what has been called the Green Room ever since.

The remains of Abraham Lincoln's 11-year-old son Willie, who died probably of typhoid upstairs in what we know today as the Lincoln Bed, on February 20, 1862, were brought to the Green Room for embalming, and his heartbroken father remained in the room while the little boy's funeral was held in the adjacent East Room.

A colossal-size portrait of First Lady Lucy Hayes was hung on the west wall in 1881 and was there for many years. Mrs. Hayes, probably the most admired woman in America in her time, is remembered for banning alcohol from the White House. Although the diplomatic community dismissed her abstinence snobbishly as a

Opposite: The Green Room, first made green by President Monroe in 1818, was often redecorated through the nineteenth century, reaching a certain "French" panache under President Grant in 1870. Lighted by gas and warmed by a central air system, this room, like the other state parlors, benefited from an air circulation device; note the registers for it high on the wall above the coal-fueled fireplace. While this black-and-white photograph, c. 1880, does not show the varied tones of the room's green colors, it ably expresses the opulence of the "Gilded Age" White House.

"practice of village society" and history teasingly remembers her as "Lemonade Lucy," an epithet never used while she lived, a large group of her admiring contemporaries contributed the portrait that was hung in her favorite room to symbolize Mrs. Hayes as the new and active public-minded woman.

Paintings in the room are today hung in "stacks" on walls that since 1902 have been covered with various green fabrics, today watermarked silk. The white Italian Carrara marble mantelpiece is one of a pair originally placed by James Monroe at each end of the State Dining Room. This one was put here and the other in the Red Room in 1902. Note that the carved goddesses who hold up the heavy mantel shelf with their heads have had their jobs eased by the sculptor with carved cushions.

The Green Room, seen here in 1932, became the first "early American" interior in the White House, of many yet to come. Working with a special committee from 1925, First Lady Grace Coolidge, and her successor Lou Hoover in 1929, endorsed the committee's idea of appearing more "American" and approved the replacement of President Theodore Roosevelt's cream-colored French-style furnishings with what they called "colonial" interiors.

With our appreciation and best wishes for a happy Christmas
1963
(John F. Kennedy)   Jacqueline Kennedy

The Green Room, completed
for President Kennedy under Mrs.
Kennedy's direction, set the tone for
state interiors today. This watercolor
of the room was used to illustrate
Mrs. Kennedy's Christmas card for
the White House staff in 1963.
Portraits of presidents and first ladies
hang on the lustrous silk wall covering,
while a variety of fabrics warm the
interior to more nearly a living room
than one can find elsewhere on the
State Floor.

Most of the furnishings of the Green Room were made in New York City in the years 1800 to 1815. Several are attributed to the workshop of the Scottish-born Manhattan cabinetmaker Duncan Phyfe. Paintings of American landscapes, genre scenes, and portraits of presidents and national notables evoke the history of the nation.

Intended for writing, sewing, or perhaps miniature painting, this tapered-form mahogany work table, one of two in the Green Room, was made in New York, possibly in Duncan Phyfe's shop, c. 1810. It is an unusual example of intricately designed and inventive cabinetwork.

Independence Hall in Philadelphia,
painted by the Danish-born artist
Ferdinand Richardt, c. 1858–60,
depicts a Philadelphia city scene with
Independence Hall in the center.

Sand Dunes at Sunset, Atlantic City by
Henry Ossawa Tanner was painted about
1885. In this serene work, one of his
largest and most ambitious, Tanner
mixed sand into the paint depicting
the dunes. The painting remained
in his family until acquired by the
White House in 1995.

THE
BLUE
ROOM

The oval Blue Room is the architectural climax of the State Floor. Situated directly opposite the North Door, it is 40 feet long, with an 18-foot ceiling. Its central location, elegant oval shape, and striking vista through the South Portico make it the principal drawing room in the White House. James Monroe, who refurnished the house in 1817 after it had been burned, acquired many pieces that are in the room today, including the gilded wood sofa and chairs and the white marble busts of Amerigo Vespucci and Christopher Columbus. Today's bordered wallpaper, sapphire blue silk draperies and upholstery, and oval blue rug are based on designs from the 1817 period. The parlor has been known as the Blue Room since Martin Van Buren's redecoration of 1837. Then, as now, it is often used for receptions, and, most Decembers, the official White House Christmas tree stands in its center.

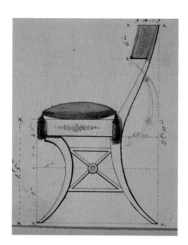

Top: The "Grecian" chair designed by the architect Benjamin Henry Latrobe for the Oval Room was a feature of President Madison's redecorations in 1809. A large suite of painted furniture in this design, inspired by furniture depicted on ancient Greek vases, was commissioned from Philadelphia and Baltimore chair makers. The room, which was in fact red and not blue at that time, was burned by British invaders in 1814. Mrs. Madison lamented the loss of Latrobe's beautiful creation.

Bottom: President James Monroe, 1820, was painted by John Vanderlyn at the White House, probably in the painter's temporary East Room studio. Enhanced with White House furnishings, the picture shows a stately Monroe at the apex of his "era of good feelings."

The shape of the elegant Blue Room, although stylishly popular when built, was probably determined by George Washington for another reason. It suited the weekly presidential levee, in which the president greeted guests formed in a circle. Washington had remodeled the rented presidential mansion in Philadelphia by making the "levee room" round-ended to serve this function. In the White House, there are two more oval rooms—the Yellow Oval Room above the Blue Room, and the Diplomatic Reception Room below it.

Jefferson discontinued the levee and other ceremonies of the Federalists, though he received the credentials of foreign diplomats in the "elliptical saloon" or "oval parlor," as the Blue Room was known until Martin Van Buren's redecoration. The room continued to be where the president most often received his guests. At the New Year's reception of 1863 Abraham Lincoln shook hands here for hours before going upstairs to his office to sign the Emancipation Proclamation.

Because of the power of its architecture, the Blue Room would be recognized today by all the presidents who have used it. Notable periods of decoration began with First Lady Dolley Madison's elegant "Grecian style," a very British fashion installed as America approached going to war with England. Her beautiful room was consumed by fire with the rest of the house during the British invasion on August 24, 1814. When he completed the rebuilding of the White House, James Monroe had agents in Paris secure fine French furniture, some of which is in the room today, and a Napoleonic-era chandelier probably very much like the present one. James Buchanan sold off Monroe's furniture, which he replaced with a very heavy gilded suite carved in flowers, the most remarkable piece of which, still in the White House collection, is a round sofa or "Ottoman" that for years stood in the center of the room. Theodore Roosevelt decorated the room in imperial blue with white-painted furniture suggesting what Monroe had put there. The current idea of reviving the Monroe period in the room originated during the administration of John F. Kennedy and has been enhanced

An official reception of the first Chinese minister to the United States was held by President Hayes in the Blue Room in 1878.

Bachelor President Cleveland, age 49, surprised the nation by announcing that he would marry his ward, Frances Folsom. The ceremony took place in the Blue Room on June 2, 1886, seven weeks before the bride's twenty-second birthday. White House florists decorated the house elaborately, not least this oval "wedding bower," where the hearth was massed with red salvia blossoms to symbolize the fire of love.

Louis Comfort Tiffany and his consortium, Associated Artists, in 1882 gave modern decor to the Blue Room for President Arthur, as a feature of their White House project. An Aesthetic vision in glazed robin's-egg blue and silver, the Arthur Blue Room conveyed the vague effect of snow falling around the edges of an overhead canopy of Union shields, woven among silver circles. President Arthur reused the Buchanan furniture of 1860, covering it in blue silk canvas.

The painter Charles Bittinger captured the Blue Room in 1903, the year after President Theodore Roosevelt tore away its Victorian look and recast it as a formal drawing room in the French Empire style. The painting captures the cobalt blue silk of the wall coverings and the sheen of the newly laid oak parquet flooring. Pieces suggestive of President Monroe's furnishings, although of larger scale than the originals, provide the historical touch President and Mrs. Roosevelt wanted.

over thirty years in the administrations of Richard Nixon, Jimmy Carter, and Bill Clinton.

The north-south axis of the city plan passes through the north door of the White House, bisects the Entrance Hall, crosses the center of the Blue Room, and continues out the center window to terminate at the Thomas Jefferson Memorial. Because it is the only room on this axis, the Blue Room assumes an importance in the city plan comparable to that of the Rotunda in the Capitol's main space, which is similarly placed on the east-west axis.

Completed a few months before
President Kennedy's death in 1963,
the newly redecorated Blue Room was
Mrs. Kennedy's favorite of all the
State Rooms. President Monroe's
purchases of French furniture in 1817
inspired Mrs. Kennedy, as they had
inspired President and Mrs. Theodore
Roosevelt, only the Kennedy Blue
Room conformed to a more nearly
classical image of a Napoleonic period
French interior than had the
Roosevelts' in 1902.

Portraits of early nineteenth-century presidents and marble busts of early explorers of the Americas, purchased for the President's House in 1817, provide insights into the early history of the country. The room's furnishings, among the most elegant and historic in the house, reflect the taste of President and Mrs. James Monroe, who lived in Paris during the Napoleonic era. He purchased a suite of gilded furniture, gilded clocks, and lighting fixtures for the Oval Room in 1817.

Left: Among the fifty-three pieces of carved and gilded furniture bought for President Monroe in Paris from Pierre-Antoine Bellangé in 1817 were two enclosed armchairs, larger than the other chairs in the suite. Made for the president and first lady, they were placed along the walls of the room, where they received their guests.

Above: The Carthaginian general Hannibal, noted for victories over the Romans in the Second Punic War, is depicted on this gilded bronze mantel clock made in 1817 in Paris by the highly skilled bronze makers Denière et Matelin.

Right: Thomas Jefferson, as vice president, sat for Rembrandt Peale in 1800, just months before he was elected president. A widely circulated engraving of this portrait became the image of Jefferson known to Americans during his presidency.

THE
RED
ROOM

The Red Room was the last of the state parlors to be named for a color, boldly decorated with red fabrics first in 1845, during the administration of James K. Polk. Today the furnishings are in the American "Empire" or "Grecian" style that was popular in the early nineteenth century and inspired originally by archaeological findings in Greece, Rome, and Egypt. Rounding out the classical theme is a marble portrait bust of a toga-draped Martin Van Buren sculpted by Hiram Powers and placed on a high shelf between the windows. The Red Room provides a richly formal setting for teas, small receptions, and meetings.

THE RED ROOM
ARCHITECTURE AND HISTORY

The historical theme of the Red Room's furniture, established during the John F. Kennedy administration, suggests the 1830s, during the presidencies of Andrew Jackson and Martin Van Buren. Most of it was made by cabinetmaking manufactories in Van Buren's native New York. Van Buren sat for the portrait bust that is now in the room, but declined the invoice. The thrifty sculptor, Vermont-born Hiram Powers, held out for his price until the president's son Abraham came up with the money. Abraham's wife Angelica often served as Van Buren's White House hostess, and her portrait, painted in 1842 by Henry Inman, hangs over a classical marble mantel acquired in 1819, originally for the State Dining Room.

The earliest view of the Red Room as illustrated in the *United States Magazine,* 1856, shows a recent redecoration under President Pierce. The walls are papered, the ceiling patterned with paint, and the windows heavily curtained.
The famous portrait of George Washington hangs here, as it would until 1929 when it was relocated by First Lady Lou Hoover to the East Room.

The Red Room has always been popular with first families and at the beginning was used as an everyday part of the house. John Adams made it a breakfast room, an informal combination sitting and eating room on the order of today's family rooms. Thomas Jefferson and James Madison converted it into a formal drawing room; in the latter case, designed by Benjamin Henry Latrobe to suit First Lady Dolley Madison's taste, it seems to have been quite fancy in bright yellow satin. This room and the adjacent Blue Room and State Dining Room were centrally heated from the basement below in 1809, when used by President and Mrs. Madison as a suite for entertaining. More than 150 years later, President and Mrs. Kennedy incorporated the suite similarly for small dinner parties and receptions. Richard Nixon served Thanksgiving Day dinner to his family in the Red Room in 1970.

Of all the rooms Louis Comfort Tiffany redecorated for President Arthur, the Red Room was his most complete. It was a jewel representing the then-modern Aesthetic taste in artistic houses. The walls and woodwork were glazed, an earthy "Pompeian red" applied undiluted at the bottom of the wall but artfully thinned as it rose to the cornice, subtly changing the wall color as it revealed other layers of color already applied beneath it. The ceiling presented a fantastic pattern of stars rendered in copper and silver.

The 1962 redecoration of the Red Room by First Lady Jacqueline Kennedy electrified the design world in the boldness of its color and the richness of its American "Empire" furnishings. For all its formality, the dramatic interior was also a cozy retreat, where, with a big fire in the fireplace and the curtains pulled shut, guests gathered after small dinners, as they had almost since the White House began.

The Lincolns sat around a table in the Red Room in the evenings, reading from piles of newspapers sent to them by mail from all over the Union, some many weeks old. In cold weather they did their reading snuggled up in wool shawls near a pitcher of water, for the dry heat that blew from nickel-plated registers beside the fireplace usually made sore throats more readily than adequate heat. President Lincoln rose from time to time and went out for war news, threading his way down the back stairs and across the lawn to the telegraph room in the War Department nearby.

In the past after a small White House dinner men retired to the Red Room for cigars and brandy, while the ladies went upstairs, joining the men again after about half an hour. It was during just such an after-dinner interlude in the Red Room in the spring of 1861 that President Lincoln first expressed to his cabinet his doubts at the advice to abandon Fort Sumter, which stood helpless in Charleston Harbor before hostile Confederate cannons. Less than a decade later, when Ulysses S. Grant's dinner guests included former Union officers, the president was likely to instigate a lively replay on the Red Room carpet of one of their Civil War battles, using lamps and vases for landmarks, the puffing cigars providing the smoke of the field.

In the traumatic aftermath of his contested election, Rutherford B. Hayes was sworn into office secretly in the Red Room on Saturday night, March 3, 1877, as, beyond the closed doors, unknowing dinner guests walked from the East Room down to the Cross Hall to the State Dining Room. Because inaugural festivities were not held on Sundays, outgoing President Grant feared a day without a president might invite trouble, so he ordered the private ceremony, the results of which were announced at dinner. In this room Eleanor Roosevelt held women-only press conferences, the first ever held by a first lady. She remembered carrying a box of candy to keep her hands from shaking but soon established warm and valuable communication with the press.

President Hayes took the oath of office in the Red Room on March 3, 1877.

American landscapes by artists Asher B. Durand, Albert Bierstadt, Alfred T. Bricher, and Martin Johnson Heade, and portraits of presidents and first ladies by Gilbert Stuart, Henry Inman, and George P. A. Healy, hang in the Red Room. The furnishings were influenced by early nineteenth-century French designs that incorporated forms and details from ancient Greece, Rome, and Egypt.

"Grecian" style sofas with painted and gilded arms and feet fashioned as dolphins were made by New York cabinetmakers influenced by English Regency and French Empire forms. This sofa was made c. 1810–25.

This center table, made in New York by French-born Charles-Honoré Lannuier, c. 1810, is modeled after French small circular tables called *gueridons*. The beautiful inlays, handsome gilt bronze mounts, and intricate marble top distinguish this masterpiece.

Left: Dolley Madison sat for Gilbert Stuart in Washington, D.C., in 1804 while her husband was secretary of state under President Jefferson. She often served as Jefferson's hostess.

Below: The grandeur of the American West is seen in *Rocky Mountain Landscape,* 1870, by the German-born artist Albert Bierstadt, who visited the area in 1863 and made studies of the dramatic scenery.

THE STATE DINING ROOM

The State Dining Room, the second largest room in the White House, is the setting for State Dinners, when a head of state is entertained, as well as for "official dinners," when the guest of honor is a prime minister, ambassador, or private citizen. The room's oak paneling, installed by Theodore Roosevelt to suggest the Georgian architecture of the 1790s when the White House was built, was badly damaged when it was removed and then reinstalled during the Truman renovation of 1948–52, and to cover the scars the walls have been painted ever since. Often displayed on the table during public tours is the monumental "plateau," a historic centerpiece of gilded bronze and mirrors acquired for the White House in 1817.

John Adams, the first occupant of the White House, used what is today the State Dining Room as a levee or assembly room, while Thomas Jefferson made it his office, which early descriptions indicate was filled with books and hobbies, even a pet mocking bird that he taught to speak. After Jefferson this was always the main dining room. The two Roosevelt presidents made their marks on the mantelpiece, the first by having American bison carved there and the second by having carved on its face John Adams's famous benediction, "I pray Heaven to bestow the best of Blessings on this House and all that shall hereafter inhabit it. May none but honest and wise men ever rule under this roof."

To one degree or another, all State and Official Dinners here follow strict protocol. Seating is by official rank. The State Department advises the first lady's social staff on what important guests can and cannot eat, what they like, who must not be seated beside whom. Once the dinners began at four in the afternoon and lasted four hours at table, no one able to rise before the president. In modern times the dinners naturally have been shorter, now about an hour and a half. Newsworthy at a State Dinner are the president's and main guest's toasts. Just before these take place, a select "pool," acting for all the press, enters the west side; special hinged pilasters swing out to reveal hidden theatrical lighting, and the press records the toast and quickly departs. The dinner continues. Among the memorable toasts in the State Dining Room was John F. Kennedy's

Top: The old dining room (1809–1902) during one of President Cleveland's State Dinners, showing the long table, which seated sixty, the formal dress of the guests, and the splendor of the elegant decorations, illuminated by the gas chandeliers and silk-shaded candles on the table.

Bottom: When the State Dining Room was enlarged in 1902, it was redesigned, with oak paneling waxed to a warm, natural color. Some of the animal heads put there in 1902 may have been bagged by Theodore Roosevelt, but most were purchased from Hart & Company in New York, which specialized in then-stylish game decorations.

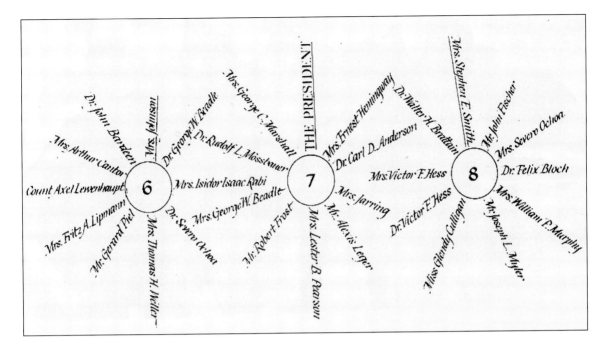

to his Nobel Prize winner guests in the spring of 1962, when he observed that this was the greatest assembly of minds ever gathered in the room since Thomas Jefferson dined there alone.

To accommodate ever more numerous guest lists, Theodore Roosevelt, about 1903, introduced individual tables for eight or ten guests in place of the traditional long table. The round tables allowed about 110 guests and packed the State Dining Room. Smaller dinners called for butting tables together into long U or T or H shapes. The detail above shows separate tables in use in April 1962, for President Kennedy's famous dinner for Nobel Prize winners.

The State Dining Room fireplace mantel bears marks of the two Roosevelt presidents: Theorore Roosevelt had American bison carved on it; Franklin Roosevelt had cut into the face of it the touching benediction of the first president to occupy the White House, John Adams.

James Monroe's gilded bronze *surtout de table* centerpiece or plateau, made in Paris in 1817, has a mirrored base and gallery of fruit and vines and figures, that extend more than 13 feet in length. It is the oldest object in continued use in the State Dining Room.

The furnishings of the State Dining Room, in place for more than one hundred years, represent the Colonial Revival style of the early twentieth century, when Americans looked back to the origins of the country and sought reproductions of furnishings to represent that idealized past. The furnishings were designed by the architectural firm of McKim, Mead & White and made by the Boston firm of A. H. Davenport in 1902.

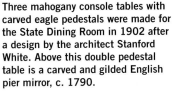

Three mahogany console tables with carved eagle pedestals were made for the State Dining Room in 1902 after a design by the architect Stanford White. Above this double pedestal table is a carved and gilded English pier mirror, c. 1790.

This image of a contemplative Abraham Lincoln hangs over the fireplace. Painted by George P. A. Healy in 1869 for a competition for an official White House portrait, it did not win and was purchased by Robert Todd Lincoln, whose widow bequeathed it to the White House in 1939. Franklin Roosevelt chose to give it prominence as the only painting in the State Dining Room.

THE
FAMILY DINING ROOM

The Family Dining Room has served as the "private" alternative to the State Dining Room for first family meals since about 1825. With the creation of an additional dining room in the private quarters on the Second Floor in 1962, this room is used primarily for official meals for a small number of guests. The elegant plasterwork and vaulted ceiling were designed for Harry S. Truman in 1948–52, following earlier neoclassical designs made for the 1902 renovation by Theodore Roosevelt. The rug, made for the room in 2008, features eagles and flower swags in the border and field medallions, all derived from the eighteenth-century French marble mantel installed in 1962. The portrait of Edith Roosevelt hanging over the sideboard was painted by Théobald Chartran soon after she moved to the White House.

Called also the "small dining room," and the "private dining room," what has been historically the everyday eating room has been largely replaced in family use by the upstairs dining room of 1962. It can be safely said that, before that, most of a president's meals were eaten in this room. The only president to use the State Dining Room for nearly all his meals was Herbert Hoover. The Lincolns ate their private meals here. A youthful guest wrote home describing dinner here with Andrew Jackson, noting that the napkins at each place were wrapped around hot bread. Almost certainly the Family Dining Room was used in 1901, when President Theodore Roosevelt, newly in office, invited the Alabama educator and political figure Booker T. Washington to "family dinner," creating a storm of racially oriented protest.

The Family Dining Room, in the 1890s, is set for either breakfast or lunch, with a brand-new "electrolier" hanging above. Against the wall, between the two pantry doors, stands a massive sideboard built in honor of First Lady Lucy Hayes and presented to the White House in 1879 by the Woman's Christian Temperance Union. Sent to auction in 1902, it was purchased for a local saloon, creating quite a public outrage.

While located on the State Floor, the Family Dining Room is not a "state" or official room, although it is used for presidential breakfasts and lunches and sometimes special dinners and meetings. It is always the staging area for the State Dining Room next door. For that purpose the furniture is removed or covered for protection, and long service trollies and warming tables are brought in with the necessary china, silver, and trays. Food is carried up from the kitchen immediately below, through the adjacent pantry, awaiting table service in the State Dining Room.

In the Theodore Roosevelt remodeling of 1902, the Family Dining Room was made to conform to the new architectural tone of the house, with a vaulted ceiling and moldings in panels on the walls. The furniture is in the Colonial Revival style of the time. Through the doors to the left can be seen the State Dining Room.

THE
GROUND
FLOOR

THE GROUND FLOOR CORRIDOR

THE LIBRARY

THE VERMEIL ROOM

THE CHINA ROOM

THE DIPLOMATIC RECEPTION ROOM

THE MAP ROOM

THE KITCHEN

THE
GROUND FLOOR CORRIDOR

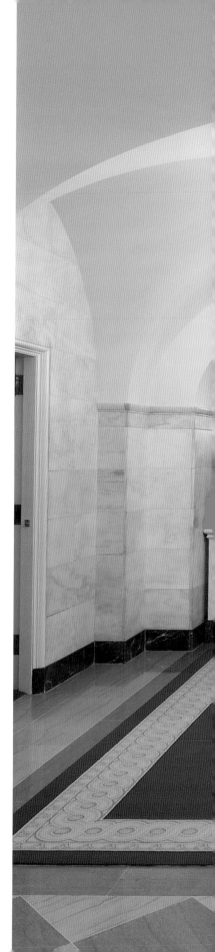

The central corridor on the Ground Floor, with its vaulted ceiling designed to support the State Floor above, is a "spine" of communication connecting all parts of the White House complex. Extending from one end of the house to the other, the corridor is kept fairly clear of furniture so that it may serve as a thoroughfare for the first family, their guests, and the White House staff. Descending from the private quarters either by elevator or stairs, the president is likely to pass through the corridor to the West Colonnade and on to the Oval Office in the West Wing. In the opposite direction is a similar path for the first lady to reach her offices in the East Wing. Tour visitors and most guests for social events first enter the house itself from the East Wing by way of this stunning corridor lined with statuary busts of America's Founders and framed portraits of first ladies.

In the house as built, the Ground Floor Corridor was "the basement," a dingy passage between service rooms, flanked by a meat room, drying room, spice cabinet, housekeeper's room, and various other domestic necessities, along with the huge kitchen and its double fireplaces. The floors were brick pavers set unmortared in sand. Natural light entered only when doors were open to the rooms along the sides, or through the doors at each end. In the early days people who lingered here carried candles in lamps, even in daytime.

The corridor's massive groin vaulting and arching were originally built to support heavy marble floors planned for the Entrance Hall and Cross Hall above. The groin vaulting is created by the intersection of pier-supported arches running north-south and east-west. The technique of such cross-arch supports developed in ancient times as crucial support in solid masonry construction. Here it assured security for the parlor floors above. When budget considerations substituted wood for the planned marble floors, the vaulting was already in place.

When Theodore Roosevelt remodeled the White House in 1902, the vaulting and arching were retained for their beauty, although, by this time in construction generally, structural steel had replaced masonry. Groin vaulting was more often an ornament than a structural necessity. Where the brick arches were broken, they were replaced in plaster. When Harry S. Truman restored the house in 1948–52, a new steel inner skeleton was inserted for support, but still the vaulting and arching were retained, today entirely of plaster.

The Ground Floor's dramatic groin vaults, seen here in the process of demolition in 1948, originally sprang over the basement's central corridor. Renovations of 1902 and 1948–52 took away the last of the original stone and brick, which was replaced by structural steel, while the historic design was replicated in plasterwork.

President Theodore Roosevelt's renovations of 1902 brought new life and importance to the Ground Floor Corridor, which had been merely a utilitarian passage. He built the stairs (right) that lead to the State Floor above. The corridor is pictured here about 1910, showing the Arts and Crafts–style cabinets that displayed historic White House china. The portrait (right) of Julia Gardiner Tyler, the second wife of President Tyler, was the first of a president's wife to be acquired for the White House.

The tradition of displaying portraits of first ladies in the Ground Floor Corridor was suggested by First Lady Edith Roosevelt in 1902. Sèvres porcelain busts of George Washington, Benjamin Franklin, and Thomas Jefferson after the French sculptor Jean-Antoine Houdon, and Abraham Lincoln after Leonard Volk, are located at the center of the hall. They were gifts from the French Republic in the early twentieth century.

Elizabeth (Betty) Ford sat for Felix de Cossio at the Fords' Vail, Colorado, home in 1977.

Rosalynn Carter posed for George Augusta at Blair House, the President's Guest House, in 1984, three years after her husband left office.

Barbara Bush chose Pennsylvania artist Charles A. Fagan to paint her portrait in 2005. Her Springer Spaniel, Millie, can be seen at left.

Hillary Rodham Clinton selected Simmie Knox to paint her portrait and posed for him in 2003. On the table is her book *It Takes a Village* and a plate from the White House Clinton state service.

Opposite: Nancy Reagan was portrayed by artist Aaron Shikler in the Red Room. She wears her favorite color, red.

THE LIBRARY

The Library, a warm and inviting space, is one of the first rooms that tour or event guests see upon entering the White House. Premier among its furniture is a suite of chairs and settees made by Duncan Phyfe, c. 1810, that was acquired in 1961 for the room by First Lady Jacqueline Kennedy. The pair of chairs before the fireplace was made locally for the White House, by William King in 1817. The red color of the painted wooden chandelier, once in the Cooperstown, New York, home of the family of American author James Fenimore Cooper, inspired the color of the shelves and fabrics in a 2007 refurbishing.

While the tradition of having a library at the White House extends back to the administration of Millard Fillmore in 1850–51, there was no room exclusively devoted to the library purpose until 1935, when Franklin D. Roosevelt created the present Library in what had been an anteroom adjacent to the men's restroom. Roosevelt supervised the design of the bookcases, which were much like those seen today, although the current ones were created during the Truman renovation, 1948–52, using old White House timbers, the natural pine left unpainted. The Library was painted and refurnished during the Kennedy administration, then redecorated in color and fabrics during the Ford administration and most recently under George W. Bush.

The several thousand books in the bookcases provide the White House with volumes that reflect American history, thought, and tradition. Located on the Ground

President Franklin D. Roosevelt, in 1935, met with the White House architect, Lorenzo S. Winslow, to plan a library in a former storage room. The result, seen here, was completed the next year. Under the president's watchful eye, Winslow designed the Georgian-style wood paneling, a compatible mantel, and bookcases with protective, wood-framed wire doors. For the fireplace surround, Roosevelt acquired blue-and-white Delft tiles with scenes of Washington's public buildings. Moderne lighting fixtures of aluminum, old White House furniture, and a rug formerly in the Green Room completed the setting.

Floor Corridor, the Library is convenient for frequent use by White House residents and staff. Now and then it is the scene of a meeting or interview, and the president occasionally televises speeches before the fireplace.

In 1977 President Carter selected the Library as the setting for his strong address to the nation on the subject of energy. Wearing a sweater, seated before a wood fire, the president opened Americans' eyes to the realities of the energy crisis.

The Library is furnished in the style of the Federal period (1790–1820) with a suite of mahogany caned and reeded furniture made in the New York workshop of Duncan Phyfe, c. 1810. A New York looking glass, c. 1810, has a gilded architectural frame and a glass panel with an American eagle painted on the reverse.

Mountain at Bear Lake—Taos was painted by Georgia O'Keeffe in 1930 shortly after she first visited New Mexico. Kept by O'Keeffe until her death, this work depicts a sacred site on the Taos Pueblo lands not accessible to the public.

Clocks in the unusual shape of a lighthouse were made by Simon Willard and Son of Roxbury, Massachusetts. This clock, made about 1825, is the only one ornamented with a portrait of the Marquis de Lafayette, who was entertained in the White House in 1824 and 1825.

Opposite: President Monroe received a delegation of American Indians from the West in 1822 and presented each male with a silver peace medal bearing his likeness. While in Washington, D.C., they sat for Charles Bird King, who went on to paint more than two hundred portraits of Indian delegations that came to the capital. Five of these portraits now hang in the Library. Shown here, clockwise from top left, are: Monchousia (White Plume), Kansa; Sharitarish (Wicked Chief), Pawnee; Shaumonekusse (Prairie Wolf), Oto; and the lone woman in the delegation, Hayne Hudjihini (Eagle of Delight), Oto.

THE
VERMEIL
ROOM

The White House collection of gilded silver, or vermeil, gives its name to this room. Received as a bequest during the Eisenhower administration in 1957, the collection continues to be displayed here, with a selection in two cabinets flanking the fireplace. During the Truman renovation the room, like others on the Ground Floor, was paneled with old White House pine milled from massive timbers used in the 1817 rebuilding of the house. Portraits of twentieth-century first ladies that are hung here include Eleanor Roosevelt, Jacqueline Kennedy, Patricia Nixon, and Lady Bird Johnson. The mahogany center table was acquired for the East Room in 1829 by Andrew Jackson.

Opposite: The White House collection of more than 1,500 vermeil objects includes French pieces by Jean Baptiste-Claude Odiot and works by English silversmiths Paul Storr and Philip Rundell as well as twentieth-century American pieces by Gorham and Tiffany. Some were made for English and French royal families such as King George II of England and King Louis XV of France.

This remarkable collection of vases, ornaments, and table service pieces of the gold-plated silver known as vermeil was bequeathed to the White House by Margaret Thompson Biddle, an American living in Paris. These Continental and British luxury objects from the late eighteenth and early nineteenth centuries demonstrate the skill of the craftsmen who formed them in clay, cast them in silver, then covered them with 24-carat gold. They relate to earlier, similar objects brought to the White House in 1817 by James Monroe, including the Hannibal and Minerva clocks and the great dining room plateau, made of gilded bronze.

The objects of the Vermeil Room are not mere museum exhibits but are used for service at dinners and as vases for flower arrangments.

The many facets of Eleanor Roosevelt are depicted in her portrait painted by Douglas Chandor in 1949. She inscribed it in the upper-right corner: A trial made pleasant by the painter.

This poignant portrait of Patricia Nixon was painted by Henriette Wyeth at the Nixons' San Clemente, California, home in 1978.

THE
CHINA
ROOM

Since 1917, the China Room has been used as an exhibition space for examples of ceramics, glass, and silver used in the White House or owned by the first families. Not every president ordered a "state service"—china designed for official entertaining. Beginning with James Monroe in 1817, the nineteenth-century state services were made in France; the 1903 Theodore Roosevelt china was made by Wedgwood in England. Since 1918, with the Woodrow Wilson china, state services have been of American manufacture. The portrait of First Lady Grace Coolidge has hung in the room since 1952; the red of her dress provided design inspiration during the Kennedy administration when the display cabinets were lined in red velvet. The French marble mantel, c. 1825, was installed in 1962.

While the China Room has served its present museum purpose for nearly a century, it was for years before that servants' living quarters, with a sunny window to the south. In 1902 it, like the Library across the hall, became an anteroom to a restroom. The clear fielded paneling in this room and other rooms of the Ground Floor are from the Truman Renovation, and in 1950s' taste were left bare, aging to a pumpkin color until painted in the 1960s.

White House table china, used constantly, does not last long. Very large dinner services in a very few years must be either replicated or replaced. The first to take an interest in collecting remnant pieces of the historic china used at the White House was First Lady Caroline Harrison. About 1890 she began assembling old tableware scattered through the pantries and attic. After her sudden death in

The "Wild Turkey" game platter is part of the Hayes state service, which was the first presidential china designed by an American artist to expressly showcase American plants, fowl, game, and marine life.

the White House in 1892, the collecting was taken up by the antiquarian Abby Gunn Baker. First Lady Edith Roosevelt, a devoted collector of antiques, shared Baker's interests and encouraged exhibiting the china for the visiting public to see. The collection was kept in glass bookcases in the Ground Floor Corridor until First Lady Edith Wilson designated the China Room in 1917. Since then the collection has grown very large, forming a timeline of the presidency through presidential taste in tableware.

When the China Room was first established as a place to display historic White House tableware, it was equipped rather like a pantry with glass-front cabinets to hold the collections. The collections eventually outgrew the cabinets, as is nearly the case in this 1920s image, so the approach was changed to showing part of the china and storing the rest, a policy followed with the China Room today.

Every president since George Washington is represented in the China Room, either in a personal or state service of glass, porcelain, or silver. In some cases a president used tableware from a previous president's selection, thus some objects represent two or even three presidents. French services of Presidents Washington, John Adams, Monroe, Jackson, Lincoln, Grant, and Hayes, English tableware from the Cleveland and Theodore Roosevelt eras, and nineteenth- and twentieth-century American-made glassware and tableware since World War I reveal the changing tastes of presidential families.

A French neoclassical silver cruet stand, one of a pair, reflects the fondness of early presidents for French objects. Made in Paris by Roch-Louis Dany in 1789, the stand was purchased by James and Dolley Madison from James Monroe in 1803.

President and Mrs. Polk ordered a rococo French dinner and dessert service decorated with the shield from the Great Seal of the United States in 1846. Edouard Honoré in Paris made the service with hand-painted flowers on the apple green dessert plates.

First Lady Mary Todd Lincoln selected a French porcelain dinner and dessert service in 1861, decorated in her favorite solferino purple color. Made by Haviland and Company, the plates were decorated by E. V. Haughwout in New York. The service was reordered several times by succeeding administrations.

The Woodrow Wilson state service was the first White House service made in the United States and the first to bear the arms of the presidential seal rather than the Great Seal of the United States. In 1918, First Lady Edith Wilson ordered the service from Lenox China in Trenton, New Jersey, one of the first companies in the country to produce high-quality dinnerware.

First Lady Hillary Rodham Clinton was inspired by White House architectural details for the Lenox state service made to commemorate the two-hundredth anniversary of the White House in 2000. For the first time, images of the White House were used—the north view on the gilded service plates and the south view on the yellow-bordered dessert plates.

First Lady Laura Bush looked to services used by former presidential families for the state service made by Lenox in 2008. The latticework border of the service plate was inspired by a service associated with First Lady Dolley Madison; the gilded eagle in the center is based on a wooden inlay design in an early New England sideboard once owned by Daniel Webster.

THE
DIPLOMATIC RECEPTION ROOM

The Diplomatic Reception Room was created in the 1902 Theodore Roosevelt renovation for use as a formal entrance for visiting dignitaries and members of the Washington diplomatic corps. It is also the principal entrance for the first family and their personal guests. Furniture in the American Federal style was placed in the room in 1960 by First Lady Mamie Eisenhower. The rug features an American eagle design derived from the c. 1817 White House china for James Monroe and a border of emblems from the fifty states, arranged in the order of their admission to the Union.

THE DIPLOMATIC
RECEPTION ROOM
ARCHITECTURE AND HISTORY

Situated directly beneath the Blue Room, and in the same oval shape, the Diplomatic Reception Room was remodeled in the 1902 renovations from a furnace room. In the original house it was the servants' hall, where domestic employees gathered around a great central table and did various duties, awaiting the jingle from a bell on the wall summoning them to rooms upstairs. The first permanent White House furnace was installed here in 1837, and the oval room served for furnaces until 1902, when it entered a new life welcoming diplomats from nations around the globe to the new American world power. Today's interior was redesigned as part of the 1948–52 Truman renovation, following a neo-Georgian motif, updated with soft-edged Art Moderne details that show the architect Lorenzo S. Winslow's commitment to design in his own time. As a reception room this space receives foreign dignitaries and visitors from the diplomatic corps who are driven by automobile to the awning leading out from beneath the South Portico. Here they find a moment of reprive to adjust a tie or shed a coat. They find restrooms to either side. Then they go to join the president elsewhere in the White House.

Franklin D. Roosevelt's "fireside chats," the radio addresses by which he calmed the troubled nation during the Depression, were usually broadcast from the Diplomatic Reception Room. Though his audience could not see him, it troubled the president that the fireplace by which he sat was not a working fireplace, so Winslow had the bricks knocked out and the old flue rebuilt, to accommodate fires once again.

First Lady Mamie Eisenhower furnished the room in 1960, with the assistance and support of the National Society of Interior Designers.

Above: President Franklin D. Roosevelt's fireside chats usually took place in this room, reaching millions of Americans in a friendly, conversational manner by which the president simplified the complexities of his solutions to the Depression and calmed the nation's fears.

Left: Before his inauguration, President Clinton asked all America to come to call at the White House, and, the day after he was inaugurated in 1993, a goodly number did. Facing C-SPAN cameras, he and Vice President Al Gore stood before the fireplace in the Diplomatic Reception Room cheerfully receiving and shaking hands with thousands of visitors who entered, single file, beneath the South Portico. Commentators at the time speculated that it was the biggest turnout since President Jackson's famous inaugural in 1829, and far more dignified.

First Lady Mamie Eisenhower accepted a substantial donation of American Federal-style furniture for the Diplomatic Reception Room in 1960. These objects, made in New York and New England, have been supplemented over the years. They were the beginning of a museum-quality collection of furnishings for the White House.

Bearing the label of its maker, the Scottish-born John Shaw, the most prominent cabinetmaker in Annapolis, Maryland, and the date 1797, this desk-bookcase has a delicately carved and pierced pediment and an inlaid conch shell on the writing board.

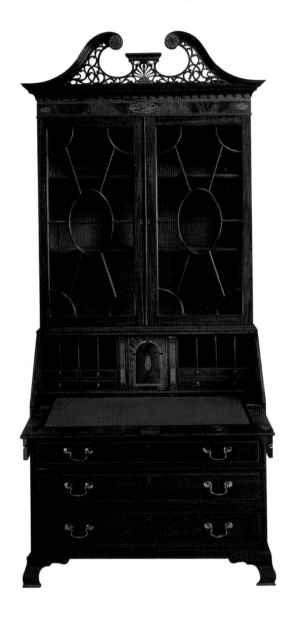

Opposite: A set of French wallpaper, "Views of North America," produced by Jean Zuber and Company in France, 1834–36, was installed in the Diplomatic Reception Room in 1961 under the direction of First Lady Jacqueline Kennedy. This woodblock-printed paper with scenes of Boston, Niagara Falls, West Point, the Natural Bridge of Virginia, and New York Harbor was based on French engravings published in the 1820s.

THE
MAP
ROOM

Shortly after the attack on Pearl Harbor in 1941, this room, opposite the president's elevator, was converted into a top-secret situation or "Map Room" in which Franklin D. Roosevelt could monitor the campaigns of World War II and receive and send sensitive communications. Today it is a sitting room with furniture in the Chippendale style, c. 1760–80, like that used in the first presidential residences in New York and Philadelphia. The paneling was added during the Truman renovation, when many rooms on the Ground Floor were paneled with old White House pine. Today maps on the walls recall the room's most famous purpose.

Before it was the Map Room, this Ground Floor room was a dressy, plaster-walled "powder room" for the women's restroom, adjacent to the Diplomatic Reception Room. At the beginning of World War II, Franklin D. Roosevelt, wanting a communications center, commissioned the film actor and producer Robert Montgomery, then Lieutenant Montgomery, to devise such a place at the White House, staffed by the navy, for the president's use. In an overnight transformation, the ladies' anteroom was invaded by a web of wires serving telephone and telegraph. Metal office desks and file cabinets were installed, and the room's walls were affixed with current maps on which were marked the locations of American ships and forces.

After 1945, the Map Room was dismantled, and its wartime appearance preserved only in memory. Here artist William Gemmell envisions what it looked like in use, during World War II, based on the recollections of Ensign George Elsey, who served in the room.

During the Spanish-American War, nearly fifty years before, William McKinley had created such a room upstairs, in a much earlier era of technology, and British Prime Minister Winston Churchill had made a temporary communications headquarters in the White House Treaty Room when he visited in 1941. Roosevelt took inspiration from these precedents, and soon his Map Room linked the president to the war zones in Europe and in Asia. FDR, delighted by its convenience and information, was likely to visit it any time of the day, and sometimes late at night might appear, pushed along in his wheelchair by a visiting Winston Churchill.

At the request of Richard Nixon in 1970, the room was refurbished as a private sitting room that the president or first lady could use for meetings, especially during the hours when the other Ground and State Floor Rooms were open for public tours.

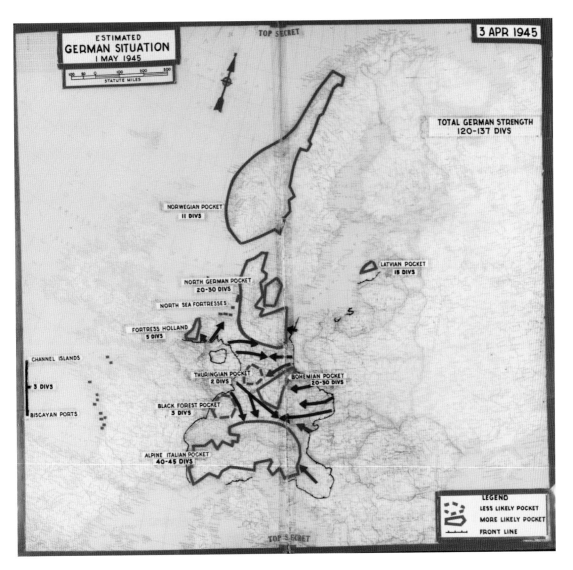

ESTIMATED
GERMAN SITUATION
I MAY 1945

100 50 0   100   200   300
STATUTE MILES

TOP SECRET

3 APR 1945

TOTAL GERMAN STRENGTH
120-137 DIVS

NORWEGIAN POCKET
11 DIVS

LATVIAN POCKET
15 DIVS

NORTH GERMAN POCKET
20-30 DIVS

NORTH SEA FORTRESSES

FORTRESS HOLLAND
5 DIVS

CHANNEL ISLANDS

3 DIVS

BISCAYAN PORTS

THURINGIAN POCKET
2 DIVS

BOHEMIAN POCKET
20-30 DIVS

BLACK FOREST POCKET
3 DIVS

ALPINE ITALIAN POCKET
40-45 DIVS

LEGEND
LESS LIKELY POCKET
MORE LIKELY POCKET
FRONT LINE

TOP SECRET

During World War II, many maps were marked up in the course of a day. Most have vanished, but this one was saved by Ensign George Elsey, who worked in FDR's Map Room and after the war pulled it from a pile of maps scheduled to be burned. In his memoirs Elsey described this map as being marked up in early April 1945, and sent to Warm Springs, Georgia, where the president was resting. It was the last war map that Roosevelt saw before his death on April 12. Elsey presented it to the White House during the Clinton administration, saying, "It deserved to survive."

THE
KITCHEN

The White House kitchen is relatively small, considering the tremendous volume of cooking that takes place in it. There actually are several kitchen rooms, the largest divided into work stations for different chefs and assistants. The pantry adjoining the kitchen has an elevator, small spiral stair, and dumbwaiter that connect it to the State Floor and a mezzanine or intermediate level where confectionery and baking take place. Ambitious menus come from these tight spaces, for every sort of occasion from a small lunch calling for turkey sandwiches to a full-scale State Dinner with four courses. White House desserts, prepared in the tiny mezzanine quarters, are legendary.

THE KITCHEN
ARCHITECTURE AND HISTORY

The basement kitchen is shown here in the early twentieth century, after being remodeled during the Theodore Roosevelt administration and further updated under President Taft.

Rare has been the time when the White House kitchen was not in use. In early days the fire never went out in the large cooking fireplaces at the east and west ends of the 40-foot space beneath heavy, low-springing masonry arches that supported the Entrance Hall above. Thomas Jefferson first modernized this kitchen in 1801, with the addition of an iron range. In 1814, the range was pulled up from the burned-out White House and cleaned of ashes to give years more of use. Those were the days when the cooks had no thermometers or other ways to measure

heat and had to rely upon their personal skills to honor such demands as for fine sugared hams, cheese soufflés, and of course the ice cream wrapped in hot pastry, of which First Lady Dolley Madison was very proud. In the 1860s, the stove was converted from wood to gas, making it easier to regulate the heat.

By this time, space for a second or "family" kitchen had been set up in the basement to the west of the original, which was now used only for the big dinners often cooked and served by caterers. Thrift-minded presidents, cautious about the staggering costs of running the White House, learned early that cooking very fine eight-course dinners for fifty to eighty people was a specialty not required every day, nor was providing light refreshment for several thousand at a reception.

During the Theodore Roosevelt renovation of 1902, the "family" kitchen was converted into a single, modern unit, with pantries, built-in cabinets, and a gas range like one in a hotel. Refrigerators and every kind of mechanical aid helped conserve space, and, as with kitchens generally, not many years passed before they were all outdated. At First Lady Eleanor Roosevelt's instigation, President Franklin Roosevelt had the kitchen rebuilt and reequipped to modern standards before World War II. Rebuilt in the renovation of 1948–52, the Truman kitchen was even more efficient. In 1969, Richard M. Nixon commissioned a major remodeling, again following the most recent concepts of efficiency. Between the milestones, the small changes are constant—a new gadget for cutting onions, a better rack for pots, a better refrigerator, a new ice cream mold, a deeper bowl. The White House kitchen today will not be the same tomorrow. Old household inventories of the presidents show it has always been updated repeatedly.

THE
SECOND
FLOOR

THE EAST SITTING HALL

THE QUEENS' BEDROOM

THE QUEENS' SITTING ROOM

THE LINCOLN BEDROOM

THE LINCOLN SITTING ROOM

THE TREATY ROOM

THE CENTER HALL

THE NORTH CORRIDOR

THE YELLOW OVAL ROOM

THE PRESIDENT'S DINING ROOM

THE WEST SITTING HALL

THE
EAST
SITTING
HALL

To celebrate the Historic Guide's *fiftieth-anniversary edition, photographs from the earlier editions have been selected to open the Second Floor chapters. This selection of photographs displays the various ways first families since the 1960s have arranged their private spaces to suit their lives and tastes.*

The east end of the Second Floor is designated the East Sitting Hall. Like the West Sitting Hall at the opposite end of the house, it has a magnificent fan window, an enduring feature of the original home. The cut-glass chandelier, made in London, is one of five English chandeliers that hang in a row down the long corridor that runs through the center of the Second Floor. The view here is from the George W. Bush administration. It features a mahogany center table, one of three acquired for Andrew Jackson's use in the 1829 East Room.

Before 1902, when the president's office was still in the White House, the East Sitting Hall served as a waiting room for callers. In this newspaper illustration published during the Civil War, President Lincoln's appointments crowd the hall outside the closed doors to the offices of the president and his secretaries, each caller with a permit issued at the north entrance downstairs.

The East Sitting Hall was the first part of the Second Floor's central corridor to be used as a room. Beginning around 1830 it was set off as a waiting room outside the president's office, which was then housed entirely in today's Lincoln Bedroom. James K. Polk set up tables here in 1846, where clerks copied by hand the message to Congress about the commencement of war with Mexico. During the Civil War era the room, used for callers awaiting appointments, had an oilcloth floor covering and was lined with cane-bottom chairs and spittoons. Here government officials, favor-seekers, and newspaper reporters joined a seemingly endless flow of humanity eager for a moment with the president. The hall continued as a reception area until the offices were moved to the new West Wing in 1902 and it entered a more genteel life as a sitting room, first used by Theodore Roosevelt's daughter Alice.

Because the 22-foot ceiling of the East Room, below, is higher than the ceilings of the other State Rooms, the floor in the East Sitting Hall is 4 feet above the floors of the rest of the family quarters. For 130 years one climbed a few steps into this space. Then, to accommodate Franklin D. Roosevelt's wheelchair, a temporary ramp was installed, and it was made permanent during the Truman renovation.

This photograph reveals the East Room below the East Sitting Hall area. It was taken from the Second Floor toward the east side fan window as steel beams were installed during Theodore Roosevelt's renovation of 1902.

Displayed in the East Sitting Hall are several important paintings depicting the varied American landscape by noted nineteenth-century artists and finely crafted furnishings made in New York, Philadelphia, and Massachusetts between 1760 and 1830.

Made in Boston, c. 1795–1810, by the English-born father/son cabinetmakers, John and Thomas Seymour, this rare lady's writing desk has tambour shutters inlaid with a drapery design, a specialty of the Seymours.

Scenes of New England are well represented in the White House. The sublime coastal scene *Sailing Off the Coast* by Martin J. Heade, completed in 1869, is a contemplative view of sails at sunset. *In the White Mountains, New Hampshire* was painted by William Sonntag in 1876 after sketches done near his summer home.

THE
QUEENS'
BEDROOM

The Queens' Bedroom, once called the Rose Bedroom, was refurbished in 2006, during the George W. Bush administration, with a deeper rose color on the walls and new floral fabrics that complement the mid-nineteenth-century Hereke rug that has long been in the room. Most of the art and furnishings were retained, including the Empire-style bed, thought to have belonged to Andrew Jackson and donated to the White House during Theodore Roosevelt's presidency. On the mantel is a *trumeau*—a mirror and painting framed together—presented by Princess Elizabeth of Britain, who would become one of seven reigning queens to stay in this room. With its adjacent sitting room, the Queens' serves as one of two principal guest suites for distinguished visitors.

Near the northeast corner of the Second Floor, the Queens' Bedroom has had many uses in the past, including that of a painters' studio, favored by the cold north light. Ralph E. W. Earl, a member of Andrew Jackson's household, once occupied this room and painted here many of his compelling portraits of Jackson and the members of his "court." It was for many years a bedroom for some member of the office staff, notably Abraham Lincoln's secretaries, George Nicolay and John Hay, until Andrew Johnson converted it into an office for clerks in his 1865 renovation and expansion of the White House office facilities. It became a guest room in Theodore Roosevelt's 1902 renovations, furnished with the present four-poster said at the time to have belonged to Andrew Jackson.

The Queens' Bedroom is remembered today for the visiting royalty who were guests and slept in it: Queen Wilhelmina and Queen Juliana of the Netherlands, Queen Frederika of Greece, Queen Sonya of Norway, Queen Sofia of Spain, Queen Elizabeth of Great Britain (the late queen mother), and Queen Elizabeth II. Winston Churchill usually occupied the room when he visited the White House, the first time at Christmas 1941, a few weeks after the attack on Pearl Harbor.

Emily Donelson, wife of Andrew Jackson Donelson, private secretary and chief political agent to his uncle President Jackson, served as Jackson's official hostess in the White House, where she gave birth to three children. This 1830 portrait is attributed to Ralph E. W. Earl, who painted portraits of Jackson's circle while living in what is known today as the Queens' Bedroom.

The English actress Fanny Kemble
was received in the White House by
President Jackson while she was on
a tour of the United States in 1833,
the same year she first sat for artist
Thomas Sully, who painted this
idealized portrait in 1834.

THE
QUEENS' SITTING ROOM

Unlike most of the Second Floor rooms, which have been adjusted to suit the tastes of successive first families, the Queens' Sitting Room retains the decor introduced by First Lady Jacqueline Kennedy in 1962–63. She chose to give the room a bold look, focused on Empire-style fabric and black-and-gold furniture. The walls are covered in blue-and-white cotton, printed with neo-classical motifs, that retains its jewel-like brilliance in 2000, during the William J. Clinton administration, when this photograph was taken. In the center is a European tripod tea table, decorated in imitation of Chinese lacquerware, that belonged to Mrs. Kennedy but was left for the White House on her departure in 1963.

THE
LINCOLN
BEDROOM

The Lincoln associations of this room lie in the fact that the sixteenth president used it as an office and Cabinet Room. When all the Second Floor offices were moved to the West Wing during the Theodore Roosevelt renovation, this area became part of the private family quarters. Today the Lincoln Bedroom and the adjacent Lincoln Sitting Room are used for personal guests of the president's family as well as for official guests. The high-back Lincoln Bed, purchased by First Lady Mary Todd Lincoln, is the room's defining object. The view shown here is from 2005, after the room was refurbished by First Lady Laura Bush for the first time in half a century. The gilded cornice and purple bed hangings were re-created, based on photographs and descriptions of the bed in Mrs. Lincoln's time.

Every president from John Quincy Adams through William McKinley used this room in the southeast corner of the Second Floor as his office. It was here that Lincoln met with his cabinet at a table before the white marble fireplace, and on the same table he signed the Emancipation Proclamation on New Year's Day 1863.

After Theodore Roosevelt moved the president's office to the West Wing in 1902, this room became a bedroom until 1929, when Herbert Hoover recognized its historical interest by dubbing it the "Lincoln Study," where he liked to work at night. Harry S. Truman created the Lincoln Bedroom as a guest room in 1952, installing the high-back, richly carved Lincoln Bed that had a Lincoln story all its own. The bed was among the costly furnishings Mrs. Lincoln purchased early in the Civil War that infuriated the president, who denounced both it and the

The copy of the Gettysburg Address displayed in the Lincoln Bedroom is one of five copies President Lincoln wrote out in his own hand and the only one that he titled, signed, and dated. The first two copies (now in the Library of Congress) were written for his secretaries Nicolay and Hay. The remaining three were done for charities to raise funds for Civil War soldiers. The White House copy was auctioned at a "Sanitary Fair" in Baltimore in 1864.

"damned old house" for which it was bought. Preserved in 1902 by Theodore Roosevelt, it enjoyed many years of service in the west end rooms of the family quarters before President Truman determined the present location. In 2004 the Lincoln Bedroom, having been changed very little since Truman's time, was redecorated by First Lady Laura Bush. The concept was to combine documentary details from Lincoln's office with research on the bed and other Lincoln objects to create a bedroom that captured in one room the spirit of the Great Emancipator's White House.

Such documentation as this pen-and-ink sketch by C. K. Stellwagen, dated October 1864, advised First Lady Laura Bush on decorative details for the refurbished Lincoln Bedroom. Note the curtains and wallpaper that have been replicated.

by the people, for the people, shall not perish from the earth.

Abraham Lincoln.

November 19, 1863.

First Lady Mary Todd Lincoln selected this rosewood center table, attributed to the New York cabinetmaker John Henry Belter, in 1861. Highly skilled in working with laminated wood, Belter carved vines, grape clusters, and roses for the apron and exotic birds for the legs.

Images and objects associated with the Lincoln presidency lend historic resonance to the Lincoln Bedroom. Many of the furnishings were purchased in 1861 by First Lady Mary Todd Lincoln for the Prince of Wales Room at the opposite end of the Second Floor. Others, such as the cabinet chairs bought by James K. Polk in 1846, became identified with their use in Lincoln's office.

Opposite: Widely circulated at the time, this 1866 print by Alexander Ritchie, *First Reading of the Emancipation Proclamation Before the Cabinet*, was engraved after Frances B. Carpenter's 1864 painting of the July 22, 1862, event. Carpenter's work conveys some of the most complete details of Lincoln's office and Cabinet Room.

Andrew Jackson sat for his portrait, attributed to Miner K. Kellogg, at his Tennessee home, The Hermitage, and several versions were done by the artist. This one may have come to the White House when Kellogg painted Martin Van Buren in 1840. This likeness of Jackson hung prominently over the mantel in Lincoln's office.

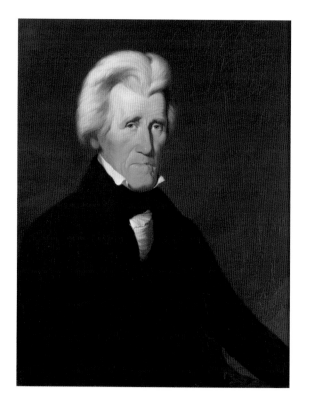

Watch Meeting – Dec. 31st 1862 – Waiting for the Hour by William T. Carlton, 1863, depicts slaves waiting for news of the Emancipation Proclamation, signed by President Lincoln on January 1, 1863. They are focused on a watch as the time nears midnight, when the proclamation would go into effect. Another version of this painting was presented to President Lincoln by the abolitionist William Lloyd Garrison, and it hung in the White House during Lincoln's years there.

THE
LINCOLN
SITTING
ROOM

The Lincoln Sitting Room serves as a parlor and dressing room for the adjacent Lincoln Bedroom. It was renovated in 2005, during the George W. Bush administration, to harmonize with the refurbishing of the bedroom. Matching carpeting, paneled wallpaper, and window hangings of the same yellow brocatelle were introduced, and the only surviving Victorian marble mantel original to the White House was installed. The chairs are all attributed to the Abraham Lincoln White House, one of them used in Lincoln's Cabinet Room. On the walls are newspaper engravings from events at the White House during Lincoln's time. This sunny and comfortable corner room recalls the style and the history of the nation under the sixteenth president.

George Nicolay, Lincoln's secretary, looked dreamily out these southeast office windows during the Civil War and counted the fireflies as he wrote to his fiancée in Illinois. Andrew Johnson, the Reconstruction president, installed the first White House telegraph in this room. The first White House telephone was placed here in 1879. Twenty years later it was the war room for William McKinley in the Spanish-American War, its walls hung with maps of the South Pacific and Caribbean. Two months before the war began, Major Benjamin F. Montgomery, the telegraph operator, had received here the news that the battleship USS *Maine* had exploded in Havana harbor, and he had crept across the dark house to waken the sleeping

President Lincoln, who had found formal photography very useful in his presidential campaign, frequently climbed the stairs of his friend Mathew Brady's photography studio on Pennsylvania Avenue. Here, on a visit November 3, 1863, he sits with his secretary George Nicolay (left) and assistant secretary John Hay.

president. Over the same telegraph in September 1901 came the news that McKinley had been shot while at the Pan-American Exposition in Buffalo, New York. Eight days later it brought the announcement of his death and the ascendancy of Theodore Roosevelt to the presidency.

Richard M. Nixon had a particular affection for this comfortable room, using it often to attend to paperwork, write speeches, and generally be alone to think. Standing in the south window one night very late, he saw student protesters on the Mall, and, to the consternation of his Secret Service detail, he joined the astonished young people, engaging them in conversation about their political and ideological views.

President McKinley used this room as his war room during the Spanish-American War. Here Major Benjamin F. Montgomery, left, works at the telegraph desk, while George Bruce Cortelyou, first assistant secretary, moves pins about on the map to denote the latest news on troop and ship locations.

THE
TREATY
ROOM

The Treaty Room was restored during the Kennedy administration to resemble the Cabinet Room of Ulysses S. Grant. The Victorian furnishings include many pieces bought for the room by Grant himself as well as others of that era used elsewhere in the White House. In this view from the Jimmy Carter administration, first published in 1979, Grant's cabinet table still occupies the center space. The deep wine-colored drapes and green-flocked velvet wallpaper are copies of Victorian designs, while the geometric border is identical to an example in the Peterson House, the house across the street from Ford's Theatre to which a fatally wounded Abraham Lincoln was carried the night he was shot.

In her restoration program for the interior of the White House, First Lady Jacqueline Kennedy converted this room from presidential study to the Treaty Room and named it to honor its place in American diplomatic history. It has since returned to use as a study, but retains the name. It is one of the most historic rooms in the White House. Here James Monroe is believed to have composed the Monroe Doctrine; here William McKinley witnessed, on August 12, 1898, the signing of the protocol for the subsequent Treaty of Paris that ended the Spanish-American War; here John F. Kennedy, on October 7, 1963, signed the seminal Limited Nuclear Test Ban Treaty between the United States and the Soviet Union; and here Richard M. Nixon, on October 3, 1972, signed the ratification of the Treaty on the Limitation of Antiballistic Missile Systems. The Treaty Room was restored in 1989 by George H. W. Bush as the president's private study, which it remains. This is one of the rooms in the family quarters likely to be redecorated in every administration, a space very intimate to the president's daily work, the home office where he studies reports, holds private meetings, and edits his speeches.

During the Hayes administration, this was the Cabinet Room. While the gas chandelier with its central pull-down table light and the giant spitoon are gone, the cabinet table is still in use in the room.

President McKinley's Cabinet Room, photographed about 1898 by Frances Benjamin Johnston, was the diplomatic setting for the emergence of the presidency to a level of power it had not known since George Washington.

The Signing of the Peace Protocol Between Spain and the United States, August 12, 1898 was painted by Theobald Chartan in 1899. It is displayed in today's Treaty Room, the same room where the event it portrays took place.

THE
CENTER
HALL

Like the Cross Hall below it on the State Floor, the Center Hall on the Second Floor provides access the length of the house, but it also serves as a drawing room for the first family and presidential guests who are received in the Yellow Oval Room. This view, looking west toward the West Sitting Hall, was made during the Clinton administration. The octagonal English partners' desk, which dates from the late eighteenth century, divides the hall into two spaces. Other furnishings, also from the late eighteenth and early nineteenth century, invite those who would just pass through to stop and sit, at least to view the paintings by American artists that first families generally choose for the walls.

The central section of the Second Floor's transverse corridor presents a long, gallery-like interior with no external light, except that which enters from the rooms along
the sides when the doors happen to be open. For most of
the first century of the house this was a dark place with
wardrobes lining the walls for storage. Servants sometimes
slept temporarily in this hall, and nurses gathered here
when sickness visited the house. Presidents' sons and
daughters found the Center Hall a fine rainy-day place to
skate and bicycle. In 1927, during a replacement of the

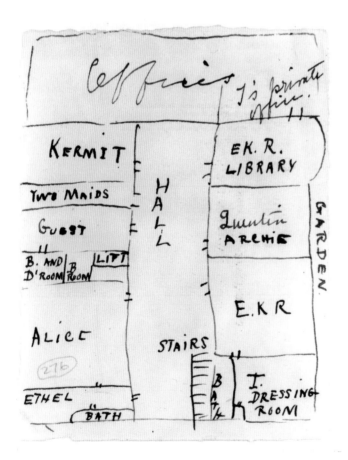

Edith Roosevelt, touring the Second Floor
of the White House after the widowed Ida
McKinley vacated it in September 1902,
made this sketch showing how she
planned to use the rooms around the
Center Hall. Quarters were cramped: left,
daughters Alice's and Ethel's rooms; the
"lift" or elevator; two domestic servants
slept in the corridor upper left. Across the
hall: the oval library top right; the boys'
room; President and Mrs. Roosevelt's
bedrooms and attached corner dressing
room, which included one of four baths
available in the family quarters. Double
doors at the upper end of the hall gave
into the president's office, Cabinet Room,
telegraph, and work rooms. The entire
Second Floor would be given to family
purposes after the West Wing offices were
built in 1902.

roof, an oculus was cut into the ceiling so daylight might fall from a large glass skylight on the newly added Third Floor, but this was closed before the 1948–52 Truman renovation, as a Civil Defense air-raid precaution during World War II. Today the space is best described as a large room of general use, still very much a passage though furnished with bookcases, a piano, comfortable chairs, and places to read and write. Guests line up in formation here with the president at state occasions, preparing to descend the Grand Staircase to "Hail to the Chief."

The Center Hall has been an essential part of the family quarters in modern times. Under President Kennedy it was furnished comfortably with slip-covered chairs, convenient tables, and books close at hand, as shown here about 1963. On the walls are George Catlin's depictions of Indian life in the West.

THE
NORTH
CORRIDOR

A narrow passage to the window over the North Door was created as a security measure in 1854 during the administration of President Franklin Pierce. It split in half one long bedroom above the Entrance Hall, leaving two rooms with the corridor between them. The North Corridor's fame lies in the view from its single window looking north across Pennsylvania Avenue to Lafayette Park. In early days it became a stage for informal presidential addresses. The most famous of them was Abraham Lincoln's on April 11, 1865, his last speech. Serenaders had gathered merrily to "call him out." With the Civil War effectively over, President Lincoln ordered the Marine Band on the porch below to play "Dixie."

THE
YELLOW
OVAL
ROOM

The family library, study, or sitting room became the Yellow Oval Room in the Kennedy administration when, as part of First Lady Jacqueline Kennedy's restoration project, it was made into a formal drawing room for the family quarters. The room also has an official function, as it is where the president greets guests of honor before State Dinners. In redecorating the room, Mrs. Kennedy chose a yellow color scheme to echo the yellow damask furnishings and curtains selected by First Lady Dolley Madison when this was the Ladies' Drawing Room. This view from the George H. W. Bush administration reveals the neoclassical furnishings and design of the plaster ceiling, in the style of King Louis XVI of France.

The Yellow Oval Room started life as a "ladies' parlor" upstairs but in use was a family room, upgraded to a library in 1850 by President Fillmore. Seen here in 1866, it is furnished with bookcases, a print trough, and other signs of intellectual pursuit.

The most formal room in the Second Floor family quarters is this elegant oval interior. When First Lady Jacqueline Kennedy restyled it as an upstairs place to entertain, it had not been a drawing room since John Quincy Adams's time in the 1820s. First Lady Abigail Fillmore created a library here in 1850, for which she received an appropriation from Congress. She housed the books in heavy bookcases, with sofas, tables, and chairs to match, and furniture of that character was added to the room for the next half a century.

The Yellow Oval Room is a historic room. From this room in 1898, late at night, President William McKinley dispatched his old friend Congressman Joe Cannon to the Capitol, to obtain funding for the Spanish-American War. Here President Franklin D. Roosevelt heard the news of Pearl Harbor on Sunday morning, December 7, 1941. For all its richness, the Yellow Oval Room is a

comfortable interior, with a fireplace always freshly laid and ready to burn. Long windows and a door open south onto the Truman Balcony, providing the first family with fresh air and beautiful views of Washington.

In the Oval Room in 1878, German-born Carl Schurz, secretary of the interior, entertains the Rutherford B. Hayes family, while below, the same room functions as a study for President Truman, with the *Resolute* desk.

THE
PRESIDENT'S
DINING
ROOM

Originally a bedroom, the President's Dining Room upstairs was one of the innovations to the family quarters during the Kennedy administration in 1961. First Lady Jacqueline Kennedy described the conversion as filling "a pressing need." This photograph of the room as she refurnished it was published in the first edition of the *Historic Guide* in 1961. The table is set with the Benjamin Harrison china, and scenic wallpaper on the walls is based on engravings of the 1820s. To complement the wallpaper, Mrs. Kennedy selected a color scheme of blues and greens. A small kitchen is adjacent to the President's Dining Room, connected by dumbwaiter to the main kitchen two floors below.

The President's Dining Room was President McKinley's bedroom in 1898, but Lincoln's great bed was replaced by a pair of brass beds considered healthful. Mrs. McKinley's handiwork is demonstrated in knitting and embroidery, while over the beds hangs a portrait of one of their two daughters, both of whom died very young.

This private dining room, with its kitchen, occupies the northwest corner of the Second Floor. With the West Sitting Hall just through the door, it forms a comfortable retreat used every day by the first family. Most family meals are eaten in the President's Dining Room, and most of the cooking is done by the White House staff, taking full advantage of the nutrition-minded chef.

When the room was still a bedroom, it was where Edward Albert, Prince of Wales and son of Queen Victoria, slept during a visit in 1860. Called the Prince of Wales Room for the next half century, the room was decorated by First Lady Mary Todd Lincoln in 1861 in princely style. She removed the old-fashioned four-poster and purchased elaborate rosewood furniture, including the famous Lincoln Bed, which she draped in purple and yellow with a frosting of white lace. Abraham Lincoln never slept in the bed, but his 11-year-old son Willie died on it in 1862, and Lincoln's body was probably laid on it briefly on the morning after his assassination in 1865. He was embalmed at its foot on a wooden "cooling board." Grover Cleveland's second daughter Esther was born in this room in 1893, unquestionably in this bed. Theodore Roosevelt's daughter Alice had her appendix removed here.

In its current use, the President's Dining Room is a busy place. Here the first family gathers for breakfast and often lunch and dinner. A hearty Gerald Ford, who famously liked to prepare at least part of his own breakfast, was the first one up in the morning and already busy at the toaster in the kitchen when the chef appeared in the doorway.

In the mid-twentieth century, the President's Dining Room was most famous as the sitting room where Margaret Truman's piano crushed through the floor, leading to the 1948–52 rebuilding of the White House.

First Lady Betty Ford found the antique French scenic wallpaper installed by Jacqueline Kennedy dark and gloomy, and had it removed. Happily it was mounted on portable linen. First Lady Rosalynn Carter had it reinstalled for its historical charm. During the Clinton administration it was hidden behind protective fabric, as it remains today.

President Lyndon B. Johnson dines with British Prime Minister Harold Wilson and Secretary of State Dean Rusk in the President's Dining Room in 1965.

THE
WEST
SITTING
HALL

Central to the family living quarters, the West Sitting Hall is dominated by a grand arched window, even larger than the one in East Sitting Hall, as the floor is not raised. Sunsets seen from this room are magnificent. The room serves as a kind of private living room for the first family, and its appearance is always tailored to their tastes. This view, from the George W. Bush administration, reflects the room's serenity. Claude Monet's *Morning on the Seine* (1897) was given to the White House in 1963 by the Kennedy family in memory of John F. Kennedy.

This is the west end of the upstairs corridor, partitioned off by a large fan-transom doorway and sliding doors. On one side of the West Sitting Hall is the president's bedroom, and on the other the President's Dining Room. Nearly always the favorite room of first families, the hall did not exist in the earliest White House but was part of the open stairwell. Ulysses S. Grant created the first actual room here in 1869 when he replaced the Grand Staircase with a new, less spacious one, and built floors over the old stairwell. In the Theodore Roosevelt renovations of 1902 the area was taken entirely into the central corridor and the Grand Staircase moved to its present location.

In 1888, First Lady Frances Folsom Cleveland was photographed by Frances Benjamin Johnston in the West Sitting Hall. With leaded glass and potted palms, it was a favorite retreat, as it remains at the White House today.

First families gather here informally with their guests. Now and again the West Sitting Hall is used for a high-level meeting.

One of Ronald Reagan's favorite parts of the White House was the view from the West Sitting Hall, with his back to the big window, looking through the long succession of rooms to the fan window at the opposite end of the house. He told his aide Michael K. Deaver that he had always dreamed of living in such a place, with "very high ceilings and white walls."

The West Sitting Hall is pictured c. 1930 during the Hoover administration. Before the Second Floor Truman balcony in 1948, the White House lacked a porch in the family quarters. A resourceful Mrs. Hoover compensated by refurnishing the hall as an ordinary American porch, with wicker chairs, a glider, comfortable chintz cushions, straw rug, seasonal flowers, and, among the potted palms, caged canary birds.

THE
WEST AND
EAST WINGS

THE WEST WING

THE OVAL OFFICE

THE CABINET ROOM

THE RECEPTION ROOM

THE ROOSEVELT ROOM

THE PRESS ROOM

THE EAST WING

THE
WEST WING

For all the serenity of its architecture, the West Wing is a hardworking office building where desk lights burn all night. Inside, the president's Oval Office and the offices for his closest advisers and staff form a maze-like plan. To accommodate the pace of the presidency, the staff is provided with dining facilities in the White House Mess, a restaurant-style basement facility, as well as a take-out. In the West Wing the president usually meets weekly with his cabinet, and every day with his most important aides. His communications center is the lower-level Situation Room, ever-upgraded with the latest technical equipment. To the mix in this beehive of activity is added the press, ever-present at the fringes of busy West Wing life.

The architecture of the West Wing complements the Georgian architecture of the main house. Discussions about building a White House office annex first began in 1882 with Chester A. Arthur and climaxed in 1900 with very extensive plans considered by William McKinley. Actually committing to office space outside the historic house fell to Theodore Roosevelt in 1902, but the first West Wing was emphatically not the president's office; it housed only his secretary and staff and was called the "Temporary Office." Tradition demanded that the president preside from the White House. In the West Wing he used the "President's Room."

The restrained, elegant West Wing structure of today, with its thin, smooth skin of stucco, contains a much larger building than appears from the outside and indeed far more a building than the first one for Theodore Roosevelt. The present West Wing in its essentials was built in 1934, using parts of the 1902 "Temporary Office." There had been many changes even to that building over the three decades following its completion. Theodore Roosevelt's successor, William Howard Taft, a brilliant manager, had doubled the size for efficiency in 1909 and built the first Oval Office. Herbert Hoover had extensive plans for an enlarged West Wing when, on Christmas Eve 1929, the building caught on fire from an undetermined source and fell to virtual destruction as the firemen's hoses froze. The fire, unarrested, blazed until morning. That being early in the Depression, Hoover decided it wise simply to "repair" or "restore" the West Wing, a symbolic decision similar to that made by James Madison in 1814, when the White House was likewise destroyed by fire. In both cases the desired result was to demonstrate survival in hard times.

Franklin D. Roosevelt took Hoover's plans, revised them,

The West Wing was completed for President Theodore Roosevelt in 1902. Built at the tip of President Jefferson's west wing, beyond the west terrace, the building was an office for the secretary to the president, not the president, who had only a work room there.

and expanded the structure in 1934 to house a much-enlarged staff. Great pains were taken, and still are, to keep the building's scale secondary to that of the White House. Cellar areas were dug out for staff offices, lighted by an atrium that on the ground above appeared to be only a fish pond. Offices were built in a low attic, which was in fact a full second floor.

The West Wing functions as a working business office for the administrator of the nation. Only the Oval Office has ceremonial purposes, but even so it is also a work space. In addition to the West Wing, the president's staff occupies the Eisenhower Executive Office Building and, across Pennsylvania Avenue, the New Executive Office Building.

President Franklin D. Roosevelt, in enlarging the West Wing, moved the Oval Office to the east, giving it access to a columned porch, which the Cabinet Room also shares. Both look out on the Rose Garden. Note the oval shape of the roof that crowns the Oval Office.

THE
OVAL
OFFICE

The Oval Office is probably the most significant space in modern history, its aura and elegance signifying the American presidency. Created in 1909 for William Howard Taft, the room was consciously modeled after the three oval rooms in the White House. The original marble mantel was retained when the room was moved to its current location during an expansion in 1934. The presidential coat of arms, redefined by Harry S. Truman in 1945, appears in a plaster relief on the ceiling, woven in the center of the 2010 rug, carved on the historic *Resolute* desk, and embroidered on the presidential flag behind the desk. The Regency-style open armchairs, made for the newly built West Wing in 1902, have been in the Oval Office since 1930.

Even after the West Wing was built in 1902, Theodore Roosevelt's working office remained upstairs in the White House, although he had the "President's Room" to the side of a large, bow-ended central office, which was that of the secretary to the president. The original West Wing was for staff. When William Howard Taft built the first Oval Office in 1909, he brought the president into architectural prominence by relocating the office in the center of the building, where the secretary had been, and to relate the new office to the White House he borrowed for it the oval shape.

Congressmen and senators often refused to meet Theodore Roosevelt in the West Wing, considering it unofficial, and instead insisted upon an appointment in the White House proper. Taft met his appointments in the Oval Office, but for ceremonies, the president still used the house. On January 6, 1912, however, he broke tradition by signing the bill for New Mexico statehood in the Oval Office. Not until Woodrow Wilson's second administration did Oval Office bill signings become usual.

Franklin D. Roosevelt rebuilt the Oval Office in 1934 when he enlarged the West Wing. Aware of the symbolic character of its positioning in the building, Roosevelt shifted the Oval Office from the center of the building to the east side. An external colonnade shaded the windows of both Oval Office and Cabinet Room and looked out on the Rose Garden, over which loomed the west wall of the White House. The Oval Office was thus oriented as it is today to relate to the historic White House.

It was Franklin D. Roosevelt who began the practice in the Oval Office of recording conversations and meetings, as a means of taking notes. This practice continued to greater or lesser degrees through the presidencies that followed, climaxing during the Watergate controversy, when tapes of conversations in the Oval Office became damaging evidence that led to Richard Nixon's resignation. The new president, Gerald R. Ford, ordered all taping equipment removed, and so many wires and instruments were pulled from the walls that the room had to be replastered and repainted.

The President's Office. White House. Washington, D. C.

The first Oval Office as shown on a postcard in about 1909, when it was completed. Green-dyed burlap wall covering, brass lamps, and mahogany furniture relate it to business offices of the time. Architectural elements were moved to the present Oval Office in 1934.

In the late 1960s, the popular names "Oval Office" and "West Wing," so-called by the press, came into common use, replacing "President's Office" and "Executive Office." Those who work here now call it "The Oval." The room has become ever more intimately associated with the president. By the 1980s the office was such a familiar background for television that it became customary to redecorate it to a greater or lesser degree for each new administration.

Some presidents actually use the Oval Office for work, while others restrict its use to high-level meetings, interviews, and ceremonies, preferring less formal and open surroundings. Dwight D. Eisenhower used the office regularly. Lyndon B. Johnson more frequently used an office on the west side of the Eisenhower Building but occupied the Oval Office the most informally, installing teletype machines, televisions, and a variety of other devices that connected him to the busy world. President Nixon had an office on the east side of the Eisenhower Building but also used the Oval Office, as did Gerald R. Ford, Jimmy

President Taft performed the first official act in the West Wing in the Oval Office on January 6, 1912, when he signed the act admitting the state of New Mexico into the Union.

Carter, and Ronald Reagan, who turned the area just outside, under a magnolia tree, into a patio sitting area. George H. W. Bush used the Oval Office but preferred more secluded space in the Eisenhower Building, while Bill Clinton spent most of his desk time in the Oval Office and, like his predecessors, gave many addresses from it. George W. Bush insisted that the men on his staff respect the Oval Office by wearing coat and tie when they entered it.

Thus within the context of the West Wing presidents have office options. Within a few steps of the Oval Office are a smaller office, a small dining room, and Reagan's shady patio where the president might work if he wishes, and space is always available in the Eisenhower Building next door. But even when not actually used for daily work, the Oval Office is never diminished in importance.

President Lyndon B. Johnson followed television news so closely that he kept a bevy of screens in action in his Oval Office. To the left of the television sets are the ticker tapes he read devotedly for news and public opinion. The shelves are filled with books borrowed from the Library of Congress.

Beyond the colonnades along the east side of the West Wing, facing the White House, a carpet of lawn bordered by seasonal flowers and blooming trees forms the Rose Garden. This scene of tranquillity can readily accommodate a crowd of 750 spectators, sometimes more, when the president uses the porch as the setting for a speech or presentation.

Presidents select images of earlier presidents and national notables as well as works of American art for this ceremonial space. Most presidents also display state gifts, special collections, and personal mementos such as family photographs. Each president chooses a historic desk for his use.

Bronco Buster was the first sculpture completed by Frederic Remington, painter of the late nineteenth-century West. Modeled in 1895 and cast about 1903, this is one of more than three hundred bronze casts of this subject. It has been displayed in the Oval Office since the 1970s.

In 1880, Queen Victoria presented President Hayes with an oak desk made from the timbers of the British ship HMS *Resolute.* A panel carved with the presidential coat of arms was added in 1945 at the request of President Franklin D. Roosevelt. The desk has been used by almost every president since its donation; President Kennedy was the first to use it in the Oval Office.

Opposite: The Avenue in the Rain is one of a series of flag-draped streets painted by Childe Hassam before and during World War I. Depicting a rainy Fifth Avenue in 1917, this impressionist work was completed shortly before the United States declared war on Germany.

THE CABINET ROOM

The long oval cabinet table, donated to the White House by Richard Nixon, seats the twenty-two members of the president's cabinet—the vice president, the fifteen department heads, and six additional officers with cabinet rank. This is twice as many members as in 1934, when the room was built in its present location. The chairs bear brass plaques naming the member's current post and any prior cabinet positions he or she may have held. The president occupies the slightly taller chair at the center of the east side, in front of the American and presidential flags. The rug, decorated with stars and olive branches, was made for the room in 2004. Portraits of four former presidents who are favorites of the current president are displayed on two walls.

Cabinet meetings ceased being held upstairs in the White House in 1902. Two cabinet rooms in the West Wing preceded this one, which was completed in 1934 for President Franklin D. Roosevelt and remains much as he built it. Here the mechanisms of distributing executive power and federal administration are refined before being exercised and put into practice. It might be called the congress-hall or forum of the executive branch of American government. To contemplate the Cabinet Room's importance is easier than trying to penetrate the details of the regular deliberations that take place in it. Cabinet meetings are rarely public, although outside, a crowd of reporters always awaits the adjournment and usually receives some carefully edited news from one of the meeting's participants.

The singular significance of the room as the top-level meeting place has rarely been rivaled by other purposes,

Theodore Roosevelt assembled his cabinet in the West Wing's old Cabinet Room for the last time on March 2, 1909. It was an ample room with a fireplace, with walls covered in green burlap and broad folding doors separating it from the "President's Room," as his office was known. The Cabinet Room was soon reconfigured in President Taft's expansion and remodeling of the office building.

although lesser activities take place in occasional spillover from crowded activity in the Oval Office, making the room seem a workplace instead of a formal assembly room. Members of Congress are likely to meet with the president here, if they come to the West Wing in a group.

At the north end of the Cabinet Room on April 12, 1945, Harry S. Truman, vice president for only eighty-two days, was sworn in as thirty-third president of the United States. Franklin D. Roosevelt had died only a few hours before in Warm Springs, Georgia. Cabinet members and officials join Mrs. Truman, gathering around the new president, as Chief Justice Harlan Fiske Stone administers the oath of office.

President Ford meets with his cabinet in the Cabinet Room on July 20, 1976.

THE
RECEPTION
ROOM

After security clearance by the Secret Service at the Pennsylvania Avenue gate, the visitor to the West Wing passes under a portico, added in 1970, and through a door opened crisply by a Marine guard, who is on post if the president is in the wing. A small hallway then opens into this intimate Reception Room, which is furnished with modern reproductions of Chippendale-style sofas and chairs. An eighteenth-century English bookcase contains the published volumes of the *Public Papers of the Presidents,* and American paintings on the walls might engage the visitor as he or she waits for an escort to an appointment in one of the West Wing offices.

Opposite: When illustrator Norman Rockwell visited the West Wing in 1943, during World War II, he captured its spirit as no one else ever has. Disparate callers wait patiently in the waiting room: the steward mans the coatroom; politicos buzz in huddles; and news reporters stampede to the pay telephones lined up in the adjacent Press Room.

West Wing visitors fall into various categories, but only a relative few come to the wing from the residence. Most enter the north door to the West Wing Reception Room. After being cleared at one of the street gates, and given a temporary pass to be worn on a long chain around the neck, the visitor proceeds up the drive or one of the walks (members of Congress and foreign visitors do not wear the ID tag). Secret Service personnel greet the visitor along the way, and in this relatively small, simply furnished interior the visitor waits for an escort to one of the West Wing offices.

Various people who pass through this room every day are "cleared," that is, they have "White House clearance." No matter who they are, even familiar employees must be cleared or approved at the outer gate, showing their permanent badge, for admission. This is true of West Wing staff, domestic staff of the house, and the press. The Reception Room serves an important security purpose in being a place where entrance in person to the West Wing is noted and where visitors may wait until their appointment begins. No off-the-street callers are admitted, a policy that began in World War II.

The entrance hall and waiting room to the West Wing, photographed in 1946, record President Franklin D. Roosevelt's remodeling. Presidential appointments usually began here with the receptionist and Secret Service clearance.

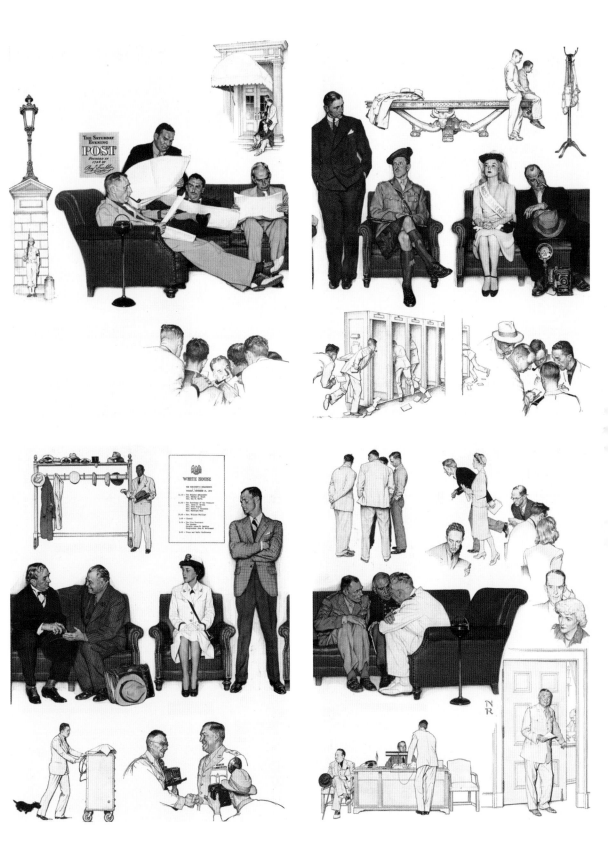

THE ROOSEVELT ROOM

This central conference room, directly across the hall from the Oval Office, was named by Richard Nixon in 1969 to honor the contributions of two major builders of the West Wing, Theodore Roosevelt who started it and Franklin D. Roosevelt who enlarged it to its present size. Portraits of both Roosevelts were placed in the room. Theodore Roosevelt is also commemorated in the room by his Nobel Peace Prize, awarded in 1906 for his mediation of the Russo-Japanese War peace settlement, and his Medal of Honor, awarded posthumously in 2001 for his heroism in the Spanish-American War in 1898. Flags of the United States, the president, the vice president, and the branches of the armed forces line the south wall. Today the room is used constantly in the course of West Wing life.

This windowless interior was created in leftover space in Franklin Roosevelt's 1934 remodeling. For many years the extra space was adapted to different purposes. President Roosevelt denoted it the "Fish Room" for his fishing trophies, and at one point he set up a tropical fish aquarium. Harry Truman, Dwight Eisenhower, and John Kennedy disliked this name. Eisenhower refused to use it, usually calling the space "that room over there." Kennedy, to give the room a better "fish" qualification, hung a mounted marlin he had caught in Acapulco on his honeymoon. The room meanwhile was used as a spillover space for small meetings and other gatherings. Callers were ushered to the Fish Room when they wished not to be seen by other callers as they awaited an appointment. Groups scheduled to see the president waited in the Fish Room before crossing to the Oval Office for a presentation or meeting.

Richard Nixon dropped the unloved name Fish Room and adopted "Roosevelt Room," taking a personal interest in illustrating the new name and converting the Roosevelt Room into a space for the reception of members of Congress and other important callers. The transformation, using portraits and memorabilia of the two Roosevelt presidents, gave new life to the room, and his staff began using it for small conferences and even business suppers with groups they needed to bring together for discussions. This use was so successful that the Roosevelt Room has rather come into its own. The president and his staff hold meetings here, and the room has proved a convenient place for the president to announce new appointments. Standing usually before the fireplace, he makes few remarks about the appointee, then the appointee steps up for a few remarks. The press records the moment, and only a minimum of office time has been interrupted. Rather more a special room of many purposes than one of specific use like the rest of the West Wing, the Roosevelt Room enjoys the prestige of being at the heart of presidential activities fully equipped for teleconferencing.

Opposite: President Kennedy's Fish Room boasted the president's fishing trophy, a television, which he called "that little gadget," and Theodore Roosevelt's original Family Dining Room table of 1890, pinch-hitting as a conference table.

THE
PRESS
ROOM

Known officially as the Press Briefing Room, today's Press Room was brought to its present state by George W. Bush, but it has been continuously updated since it was established as a permanent space by Richard Nixon in 1970. Heretofore the press, in increasingly large numbers, had assembled in the Eisenhower Building next door, unless invited into the West Wing. The room is often seen on the television news. From the platform of the Press Room the president's press secretary addresses and responds to news reporters who fill the room. When the president is at the podium, the questions and answers are broadcast to the world.

The architectural envelope of today's Press Room is the original brick structure built by Thomas Jefferson in 1808 to house his domestic service rooms and, below, his wine cellar. For more than a century the White House laundry was housed in the several rooms that opened off the colonnade. In 1934, Franklin D. Roosevelt had a pool built in this space. When Richard Nixon created a Press Room here, the interior was wholly changed, yet in the dark cellar beneath it the swimming pool survives, now filled with wiring conduit. Its blue-green tiles still shimmer when lights hit them. Along the walls dim traces of archways to the early stables and Jefferson's wine cellar can be discerned in the old brickwork.

At the White House the proximity of the press, for whatever the logistical complications, is a tremendous asset to the presidency. William McKinley envisioned the first press office in a monumental addition to the White House, drawn up in 1900, with indoor facilities for the reporters. McKinley's idea was current when he was assassinated in 1901; in the next year the "Temporary Office" or West Wing was built, with the first White House Press Room. It was not a very hospitable space, with one window, a coal-burning fireplace, a desk, and a few tables and chairs. But any disadvantages of the cramped quarters were more than compensated by the location within the White House complex, out of the rain and snow. A somewhat larger room, with telephones, resulted from the 1934 renovations.

President Franklin Roosevelt's swimming pool, completed in 1934, greatly aided in the personal battle he fought against the polio that had struck him down as a young man. Children across America contributed dimes to the fund that built the pool, and the pool was still in use until 1970, when floored over to make space for the new Press Room. The indoor pool was replaced with an outdoor pool by President Ford in 1975.

When Richard Nixon took office in 1969, he ordered the White House indoor swimming pool floored over and gave the press the best room it had ever had. It was also quickly worn by heavy use and subject to continual adaptation to accommodate innovation in technical equipment, not only with lights and cameras and recording devices, but with the appearance of the computer. While the room was improved and adjusted in small ways during the thirty-five years after Nixon, it received no comprehensive remake until 2007, under George W. Bush.

The White House Press Room is, if anything, a work space, used hard and constantly. Here President Reagan faces reporters and cameramen in a scene that has become typical in the West Wing.

THE
EAST
WING

O n the east of the central block the 1902 reconstruction of Jefferson's colonnade extends to the offices in the East Wing, a two-story building erected by President Franklin D. Roosevelt in 1942 during World War II. He had long intended the new structure for a White House museum, but the times outpaced the plan and when completed the building was quickly taken over for wartime offices. Today it provides space for the social staff, some White House security detail, and some presidential staff. It is used as the entrance for tours as well as guests for official receptions, dinners, and other official events.

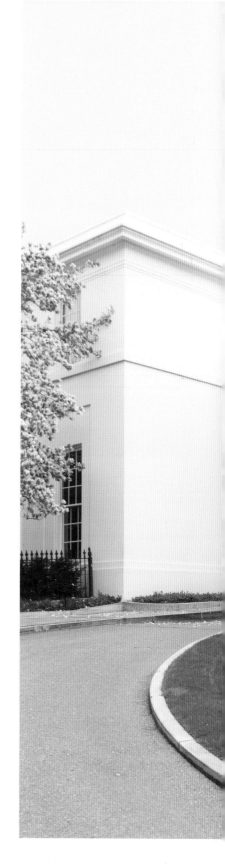

THE EAST WING
ARCHITECTURE AND HISTORY

The first east wing, long in disuse, was torn down by Andrew Johnson in 1866. Rebuilt thirty-six years later as a feature of the remodeling undertaken by President Theodore Roosevelt in 1902, the East Wing became the main business and social entrance of the house. Here the visitor is greeted by the Secret Service and proceeds into the house itself. In 1942 President Franklin D. Roosevelt added the large office block to the eastern end, creating the present entrance.

One enters the 1942 building and passes to the 1790s vaulted basement through the East Colonnade. When rebuilt from Thomas Jefferson's plan in 1902, the colonnade was intended to be open in the summer, but the glass storm windows for winter were never removed

and air-conditioning in 1952 assured that they would not. The colonnaded porch passes the movie theater (which doubles for big events as a coat room) on the left, the East Garden on the right, and enters the house directly into the Ground Floor Corridor, which is a thoroughfare linking all parts of the house and its wings.

Brick paths and boxwood borders characterize the East Garden, which was designed in 1913 to suggest a Victorian garden.

The enclosed colonnade of the East Terrace serves as a passage linking the East Wing to the Ground Floor Corridor of the house.

Between the house and the East Wing is the East Garden. President Lyndon B. Johnson named it the Jacqueline Kennedy Garden.

Since 1962, the White House Historical Association has maintained a broad-ranging publications program, which includes the following major publications.

Abraham Lincoln: Highlights of the White House Collection, 2009.

Art in the White House: A Nation's Pride by William Kloss. 2nd edition, 2008.

The First Ladies of the United States of America. 12th edition by Allida Black, 2009.

George Washington: Highlights of the White House Collection, 2008.

A Kid's Guide to the White House by Betty Debnam, 1997.

Lincoln at Home: Two Glimpses of Abraham Lincoln's Domestic Life by David Herbert Donald, 1999.

The Living White House. 12th edition by Betty C. Monkman, 2007.

Our Changing White House edited by Wendell Garrett, 1992.

The President's House: A History by William Seale. 2nd edition, 2008.

The Presidents of the United States of America. 18th edition by Michael Beschloss and Hugh Sidey, 2009.

Six Months at the White House with Abraham Lincoln by Francis Bicknell Carpenter. Illustrated reprint with introduction by Harold Holzer, 2008.

Tokens and Treasures: Gifts to Twelve Presidents by Lisa B. Auel. Facsimile edition, 2007.

The White House: The History of an American Idea by William Seale. 2nd edition, 2001.

The White House ABC: A Presidential Alphabet by John Hutton, 2004.

The White House: Actors and Observers edited by William Seale, 2002.

The White House: An Illustrated History by Catherine O'Neill Grace, 2003.

The White House: Celebrating Two Hundred Years, 2002.

The White House Easter Egg Roll by C. L. Arbelbide, with illustrations by Barbara Leonard Gibson, 1997.

The White House: The First 200 Years edited by Frank Freidel and William Penack, 1994.

The White House Garden by William Seale, 1996.

The White House: Its Historic Furnishings and First Families by Betty C. Monkman, 2000.

White House History: The Journal of the White House Historical Association. Published semi-annually from 1983 to the present.

The White House Remembered: Recollections by Presidents Richard M. Nixon, Gerald R. Ford, Jimmy Carter, and Ronald Reagan edited by Hugh Sidey, 2005.

White House Glassware: Two Centuries of Presidential Entertaining by Jane Shadel Spillman. Facsimile edition, 2007.

All images are copyrighted by the White House Historical Association (WHHA) unless listed below. All artwork and objects are in the White House Collection unless listed below, and those images are copyrighted by the WHHA.

Illustration credits key:

HABS—Historic American Buildings Survey, National Park Service

LOC—Library of Congress

NARA—National Archives

NPS—National Park Service

xii   John F. Kennedy Presidential Library and Museum

10   Rodica Prato for WHHA

14   [top left] Maryland Historical Society

14   [bottom] Mrs. John M. Scott Jr., Mobile, Alabama

20   [bottom] LOC

23   Bettmann / Corbis

26   Rodica Prato for WHHA

30   [bottom] LOC

32   Bettman / Corbis

33   [bottom] Getty Images

35   Rodica Prato for WHHA

37   Rodica Prato for WHHA

47   LOC

48   [top] William J. Clinton Presidential Library

53   [top] Rutherford B. Hayes Presidential Center

53   [bottom] Jim Watson / AFP / Getty Images

56   John F. Kennedy Presidential Library and Museum

57   Nicholas Kamm / AFP / Getty Images

61   LOC

63   [top] LOC

63   [bottom] Lyndon Baines Johnson Presidential Library and Museum

71   Rutherford B. Hayes Presidential Center

73   Collection of Nelson Pierce

80   [top] Maryland Historical Society

80   [bottom] Collection of the City of New York

81   [top] LOC

81   [middle] LOC

81   [bottom] LOC

90   Historical Society of Pennsylvania

91   LOC

92   John F. Kennedy Presidential Library and Museum

93   Rutherford B. Hayes Presidential Center

98   [bottom] LOC

99   [top] John F. Kennedy Presidential Library and Museum

104   LOC

110   Abbie Rowe, NPS, White House

111   NARA

116   Abbie Rowe, NPS, White House

117   Jimmy Carter Library

132   Anthony Stewart, National Geographic

133   [top] Bettmann / Corbis

133   [bottom] Associated Press

142   Harris and Ewing, LOC

149   Sagamore Hill National Historic Site, NPS

163   [top] Western Reserve Historical Society, Cleveland, Ohio

168   LOC

169   LOC

173   [top] LOC

176   Theodore Roosevelt Collection, Houghton Library, Harvard University

177   John F. Kennedy Presidential Library and Museum

178   Robert Kapsch, HABS

182   LOC

183   [top] LOC

183   [bottom] Abbie Rowe, NPS, White House

186   [bottom] Abbie Rowe, White House Collection

190   LOC

191   Herbert Hoover Presidential Library

196   Detroit Photographic Company, LOC

197   Abbie Rowe, NPS, White House

204   LOC

205   [top] Lyndon Baines Johnson Presidential Library and Museum

210   LOC

211   [top] Harry S. Truman Library

211   [bottom] Bettman / Corbis

214   Harry S. Truman Library

215   Printed by permission of the Norman Rockwell Family Agency. Copyright © 1943 The Norman Rockwell Family Entities. Illustration © 1943 SEPS

222   NARA

223   Ronald Reagan Library

Loan Items Pictured in This Edition

West Sitting Hall
Mending, by Daniel Garber, 1918, oil on canvas,
Private Collection

West Wing Reception Room
Washington Crossing the Delaware,
by Eastman Johnson, 1851, oil on canvas,
Alex and Marie Manoogian Foundation

Oval Office
Jar, by Steve S. (Iroquois), date unknown,
pottery, National Museum of the American
Indian, Smithsonian Institution

Bottle, Intertwining Scrolls, by Jereldine Redcorn
(Cadd), 2005, pottery, National Museum of the
American Indian, Smithsonian Institution

Register Patent Model of Morse Telegraph, by
Samuel F. B. Morse, 1849, metal and wood, National
Museum of American History, Kenneth E. Behring
Center, Smithsonian Institution

Martin Luther King, Jr., by Charles Alston,
1970, bronze, National Portrait Gallery,
Smithsonian Institution

Page numbers in bold indicate photographs and illustrations.

A

A. H. Davenport Company, 100
Adams, John, 6, 91, 98, **99**
Air Force One, 32
Andrews, E. F., 61
Andrews Air Force Base, 32
Aquia Creek, 16
arrival ceremonies, 46, 56
art work. *See* fine and decorative arts;
    paintings; prints; sculpture
    (Remington)
Arthur, Chester A., 46, 81, 196
arts, fine and decorative. *See* fine
    and decorative arts
Arts and Crafts (style), **111**
Associated Artists, 81
attic, 15, 39
Augusta, George, 112
Avenue in the Rain, The (Hassam
    painting), 206, **207**

B

Baker, Abby Gunn, 127
balustrade, stone, 15, **15**
bandstand, 32
Barlow, Joel, 70
bear cubs, 46
Beaux-Arts, École de, 29
bedrooms
    Lincoln Bedroom, 158, **158–61,**
    162–64, **163,** 166
    president's, 190
    President's Dining Room as, 186,
    186
    Queens' Bedroom, 152, **152–53,** 154
    Rose Bedroom, 152
    for servants, 152
beds
    brass beds, **186**
    Lincoln Bed, 70, 158, **158–60,** 162–
    63, 186
    in Queens' Bedroom, 152, 154
Begin, Menahem, 62
Bellangé, Pierre-Antoine, 84
Belter, John Henry, 164
Biddle, Margaret Thompson, 122
bier, **61**
Bierstadt, Albert, 94, 95

bill signings, 202
Bittinger, Charles, 82
Blair House, 32
Blue Room
    architecture, 80, 82
    description, 76, 80
    doors, 42
    first ladies and, 80, 83
    floors, 82
    furnishings and decor, 76, 80, 82, 84,
    84–85
    heating in, 91
    history, 80, 82
    paintings of, **82**
    photographs, **76–79, 81, 83, 84, 85**
    presidents and, 76, 80, 81, 82, 83, 84
    receptions in, 76, **81**
    redecorations of, 76, 80, **81**
    uses, 76, 80
    weddings in, **81**
books and bookcases, 116, **116, 134,**
    205, 212
boxwoods, 10
brass stars, 42
Breeden, Robert, **xii**
Bricher, Alfred T., 94
British invasion (1814), 16, 31, 34, 80
Bronco Buster (Remington sculpture),
    206
Buchanan, James, **60,** 80
Bush, Barbara, **112**
Bush, George H. W. (father), 172, 203
Bush, George W. (son)
    in Cross Hall, **53**
    Queen Elizabeth II and, **33**
    Library and, 116
    office space of, 203
    Oval Office and, 203–4
    Press Room and, 220, 223
    state service china, **129**
Bush, Laura, 66, 129, 158, 163
busts
    of Christopher Columbus, 76
    of Benjamin Franklin, 112
    in Ground Floor Corridor, 108, 112
    of Thomas Jefferson, 112
    in Red Room, 86, 90
    of Martin Van Buren, 86, 90
    of Amerigo Vespucci, 76
    of George Washington, 112

C

cabinet meetings, 210
Cabinet Room, 165, **172, 173,** 197,

208–11, **208–10**
Calderón, Felipe, **57**
Camp David Accords (1978), 62
candelabrum, French, **64**
Cannon, Joe, 182
Carlton, William T., 165
Carmichael, Leonard, **xii**
Carpenter, Frances B., 164
carpeting. *See* rugs and carpeting
Carter, Jimmy, 39, 62, 82, **117,** 203
Carter, Rosalynn, **112,** 187
Castro, Nash, **xii**
Catlin, George, 177
ceilings, 91, 148, 180, 198
Center Hall, 174–77, **174–76**
centerpiece (plateau), 96, **100,** 122
chairs
    in Blue Room, **84**
    cabinet chairs, 164
    Grecian chair, **80**
    in Library, 114
    in Lincoln Sitting Room, 166
    in Oval Office, 198
    in Reception Room, 212
    slip-covered chairs, **177**
    See also sofas
chandeliers
    in Blue Room, 80
    in Cabinet Room, **172**
    draped in black, 62
    in East Room, 58, 60, **63**
    in East Sitting Hall, 146, **147,** 149
    in Entrance Hall, 49
    in Library, 114
Chandor, Douglas, **122**
Chartran, Théobald, 102
Children's Garden, **26**
china, state service
    Bush (George W.), **129**
    Clinton, **129**
    collections, 126–27, **127**
    Harrison, 184–85
    Hayes, **126**
    history, 124
    Lincoln, **129**
    Madison, 129
    Monroe, 124, 130
    Polk, **128**
    presidential representation, 128
    Roosevelt (Theodore), 124
    Wilson, 124, **129**
China Room, 124–29, **124–29**
Chippendale (style), 136, 212
Christmas tree, 76

Churchill, Winston, 138, 154

city axis, 82

Civil Rights Act (1964), 62, 63

Clark, George Rogers, 20, 46

Cleveland, Esther, 186

Cleveland, Frances Folsom, **81, 190**

Cleveland, Grover, **81, 98**

Clinton, Hillary Rodham, **112, 129**

Clinton, William J., 82, **133,** 156, 187, 203

clocks, **49, 84, 118,** 122

coat of arms, presidential, 198, 206, **206**

Colonial Revival (style), 64, 100, **105**

color schemes

    Blue Room, 80

    Green Room, 66, 70

    Library, 116, 117

    President's Dining Room, 184

    Queens' Bedroom, 152

    Red Room, 86, 91, 92

    Yellow Oval Room, 180

Columbus, Christopher, 76

Common Sense (Paine), 70

Congress, 19, 60, 64, 182, 211

congressmen, 202

Conservation Conference (1908), 62

Coolidge, Calvin, 39

Coolidge, Grace, 72, 124, **125**

Cooper, James Fenimore, 114

cornices

    Cross Hall, 50

    East Room, 58, 64

    Lincoln Bedroom, 158

    modillion, 17, **17**

    window, 58, 64

Cortelyou, George Bruce, **169**

Cossio, Felix de, **112**

Cross Hall, 50, **50–53,** 52–53

cruet stand, silver, **128**

curtains

    Blue Room, 76

    Green Room, 66

    Lincoln Bedroom, 163

    Lincoln Sitting Room, 166

    Treaty Room, 170

    Yellow Oval Room, 180

D

Daniels, Clifton, **56**

Daniels, Margaret Truman, **56,** 186

Dany, Roch-Lois, 128

Deaver, Michael K., 191

decor. *See* furnishings and decor

Delano, William Adams, 29

Delft tiles, 116

Deniére et Matelin (bronze makers), 84

desks

    in Center Hall, **174–75**

    desk-bookcase, **134**

    octagonal English partners' desk, **174–75**

    Resolute desk, **183,** 198, **199, 206**

    writing desk, **150**

Dinners, State and official, **57,** 98–99

Diplomatic Reception Room, 32, 80, 130–35, **130–35**

Donelson, Andrew Jackson, 154

Donelson, Emily, **154**

doors

    Blue Room, 42

    Cabinet Room, 210

    Family Dining Room, **104**

    Green Room, 70

    North Door, 20, 22, **22,** 23, 46, 82, 178

    State Dining Room, **53, 105**

    West Sitting Hall, 190

draperies. *See* curtains

Durand, Asher B., 94

E

Eagle of Delight (Hayne Hudjihini), **119**

Earl, Ralph E. W., 154

East Colonnade, **28,** 226–27, **227**

East Entrance, **28**

East Garden, 26, **28,** 227, **227**

East Room

    ceiling, 148

    description, 58

    furnishings and decor, 58, 60, **63,** 64, **64–65**

    illustrations, **60**

    Meriwether Lewis and, 61

    photographs, **58–59, 149**

    presidential portraits in, 58, 60–61, 90

    presidents and, 22, 60, 61, **61,** 62, 63

    receptions in, 60, **60**

    renovation (1902) and, 63

    uses, 61–62

East Sitting Hall, 19, 146, **146–49,** 148, 150

East Terrace, 227

East Wing

    architecture, 226–27

    description, 224

history, 19, 226–27

illustrations, **12, 28**

photographs, **224–26**

presidents and, 19, 34, 224, 226

renovations, 34, 39, 226

uses, 19, 224

Easter Egg Roll, 32

Edward Albert (prince), 186

Eisenhower, Dwight D., 203, 218

Eisenhower, Mamie, 130, 132, 134

Eisenhower Executive Office Building, 197, 203, 204, 220

electrolier, **104**

Elizabeth (queen mother), 154

Elizabeth II (queen), **33,** 152, 154

Ellipse, 6

elm trees, 10

Elsey, George, 138, 139

Emancipation Proclamation, 80, 162, 164

Entrance Hall, 42, **42–49,** 46–49, 54, 56

entrances, 18, **18**

    See also names of individual entrances

entrances, presidential, 56

F

Fagan, Charles A., 112

Family Dining Room, 102, **102–5,** 104–5, **219**

Federal (style and period), 66, 116, 118, 130, 134

fences, 6, **8–9,** 10, 20

Fillmore, Abigail, 182

Fillmore, Millard, 29, 116, 182

fine and decorative arts

    Blue Room, 84, **84–85**

    China Room, 128, **128–29**

    Diplomatic Reception Room, 134, **134, 135**

    East Room, 64, **64–65**

    East Sitting Hall, 150, **150, 151**

    Entrance Hall, 49, **49**

    Green Room, 74, **74–75**

    Ground Floor Corridor, 112, **112, 113**

    Library, 118, **118–19**

    Lincoln Bedroom, 164, **164–65**

    Oval Office, 206, **206–7**

    Queens' Bedroom, 152

    Red Room, 94, **94, 95**

    Vermeil Room, 122, **122–23**

fire (1814), 16, 31, 34, 64, 80

fire (1929), 39, 196
Finley, David, **xii**
fireplaces
    Cabinet Room, 210
    Diplomatic Reception Room, 132
    Green Room, **71**
    kitchen, 142
    Library, **114**, **116**
    Press Room, 222
    State Dining Room, **99**
    Vermeil Room, **120**
    See also mantelpieces
fireside chats, 132, **133**
first family
    Center Hall and, 174
    Diplomatic Reception Room and, 130
    Family Dining Room and, 102
    Ground Floor Corridor and, 108
    grounds and, 4, 32
    President's Dining Room and, 186
    Truman Balcony and, 183
    West Sitting Hall and, 188
first ladies, portraits of
    Barbara Bush, **112**
    Rosalynn Carter, **112**
    Hillary Rodham Clinton, **112**
    Grace Coolidge, 124, **125**
    Betty Ford, **112**
    in Ground Floor Corridor, 108, 112
    Lady Bird Johnson, 120
    Jacqueline Kennedy, 120
    Patricia Nixon, 120, **122**
    Nancy Reagan, **113**
    Edith Roosevelt, 102, **102**
    Eleanor Roosevelt, **122**
    in Vermeil Room, 120
    Martha Washington, 61
First Reading of the Emancipation Proclamation Before the Cabinet (Ritchie print), **165**
Fish Room, 218, **219**
floors
    Blue Room, 82
    Cross Hall, 52
    Entrance Hall, 42, 46, 54
    Green Room, 70
    Ground Floor Corridor, 110
    over swimming pool, 222, 223
flowers and shrubs, 6, 10, 24, 81
Folsom, Frances (later Cleveland), **81**, **190**
Ford, Betty, **112**, 187
Ford, Gerald R., 116, 186, 202, 203, **211**, 222
formal gardens, 26

fountain, **11**
Franklin, Benjamin, 112
Frederika (queen), 154
French (style), **63**, **72**
French Empire (style), **82**, 152, 156
funeral processions, **23**
furnaces, 132
furnishings and decor
    Blue Room, 76, 80, 82, 84, **84**
    Center Hall, 174, **174–75**, 177
    Diplomatic Reception Room, 130, 132, 134
    East Room, 58, 60, **63**, 64
    East Sitting Hall, 150
    Green Room, 66, 72
    Ground Floor Corridor, **111**
    Andrew Jackson's acquisitions, 146
    Library, 114, **116**, 118
    Lincoln Bedroom, 164
    Mary Todd Lincoln's selections, 164
    for James Monroe, 84
    Oval Office, 198, **199–200**, **203**, 206, **206–7**
    Queens' Bedroom, 152
    Red Room, 86, 90, 92, 94, **94**
    State Dining Room, 96, 99, 100, **100**, **101**, 122
    Treaty Room, 170
    Vermeil Room, 120
    West Sitting Hall, 191
    White House, 134
    Yellow Oval Room, 180
    See also fine and decorative arts; *specific items; specific styles*

G

gardens
    Children's Garden, **26**
    East Garden, 26, **28**, 227, **227**
    formal gardens, 26
    Jacqueline Kennedy Garden, 28, **227**
    Kitchen Garden, **26**
    Franklin D. Roosevelt and, 26
    Rose Garden, **13**, 26, **27**, 33, 197, **205**
    vegetable garden, 6
Garrison, William Lloyd, 165
gas lamps, 21, **21**
gasoliers, 60
gates and gateposts, 10, **12**, 20, 21, **21**
Gemmell, William, 138
Generous Chief (Petaisharro), **119**
geraniums, red, 10

Gettysburg Address, **162–63**
Gore, Al, **133**
Gorham silver, 122
Grand Staircase
    architecture, 56
    description, 54
    history, 56
    photographs, **54–55**, **57**
    presidents and, 56, 190
    renovation (1902) and, 52, 56, 190
    uses, 56
Grant, Nellie, 62
Grant, Ulysses S.
    East Room and, 60
    Grand Staircase and, 190
    Green Room and, 70
    north grounds and, 10
    President's Park and, 6
    Red Room and, 93
    Treaty Room and, 170
    West Sitting Hall and, 190
Great Seal of the United States, 128, 129
Grecian (style), 80, 86, **94**
Green Room
    architecture, 70, 72, 74
    description, 66
    doors, 70
    fireplace, **71**
    first ladies and, 66, 70, 73
    floors, 70
    furnishings and decor, 66, 72, 74, **74–75**
    history, 70, 72
    illustrations, **73**
    paintings in, 74
    photographs, **66–69**, **71**, **72**
    presidential portraits in, 66, **73**
    presidents and, 70, 73
    redecorations, 70, 72
    uses, 70
groin vaulting, 110, **110**
Grosvenor, Melville Bell, **xii**
Ground Floor, **15**, 136
Ground Floor Corridor, 108, **108–13**, 110, 112, 227
grounds, 4, **4–5**, **6–7**, 32
    See also north grounds; south grounds
gueridons (table), **94**
Gugler, Eric, 29

H

"Hail to the Chief," 46, 56
Hannibal clock, **84**, 122
Harding, Warren G., 63
Harper's Weekly, 60
Harrison, Benjamin, 184–85
Harrison, Caroline, 126–27
Harrison, William Henry, 63
Hart & Company, 98
Hassam, Childe, 206, **207**
Haughwout, E. V., 129
Haviland and Company, 129
Hay, John, 154, 162, **168**
Hayes, Lucy, 70, 72, 104
Hayes, Rutherford B.
    Cabinet Room and, **172**
    Cross Hall and, **53**
    East Room meeting, **62**
    Easter Egg Roll and, 32
    illustration, **93**, **183**
    north grounds and, 10
    Oval Room and, **183**
    receptions held by, **81**
    Red Room and, 93
    Resolute desk, 206
    state service china, **126**
    Martha Washington's portrait and, 61
Hayne Hudjihini (Eagle of Delight), **119**
Heade, Martin Johnson, 94, 151
Healy, George P. A., 94, 101
heating, 70, 91, 92
    See also furnaces
Hedl, Paulus, 10
helicopter, president's, 32
Hoban, James, 7, 13, 29, 34
Honoré, Edouard, 128
Hoover, Herbert, 39, 104, 162, 196
Hoover, Lou, 72, 90, 191
Houdon, Jean-Antoine, 112

I

In the White Mountains, New Hampshire (Sonntag painting), **151**
inaugural address, **32**
inaugurations, 32, **32**, 93, 133
Independence Hall in Philadelphia (Richardt painting), **75**
Indians, 62, **62**, 118, **119**
Inman, Henry, 90, 94

It Takes a Village (Hillary Rodham Clinton), **112**

J

Jackson, Andrew
    East Room and, 60, 120
    entrances by, 56
    Family Dining Room and, 104
    furnishings acquired by, 120, 146
    north grounds and, 10
    portraits of, 154, **165**
    Vermeil Room and, 120
Jackson Magnolias, 24
Jacqueline Kennedy Garden, **28**, **227**
Jean Zuber and Company, 134
Jefferson, Thomas
    Blue Room and, 80
    bust of, 112
    East Room and, 61
    east and west wing and, 19, 29, 34
    Entrance Hall and, 46
    Grand Staircase and, 56
    Green Room and, 70
    kitchen and, 142
    Louisiana Purchase and, 20
    Marine Band and, 47
    museum of artifacts, 46
    portrait of, **84**
    President's Park and, 6
    Press Room and, 222
    Red Room and, 91
    State Dining Room and, 98
    West Colonnade and, 33
Jett, Thomas Sutton, **xii**
Johnson, Andrew, 154, 168, 226
Johnson, Lady Bird, 120
Johnson, Lynda, 62
Johnson, Lyndon B.
    Civil Rights Act (1964) and, 62, **63**
    Jacqueline Kennedy Garden and, 227
    office space of, 203
    photographs, **187**, **205**
Johnston, Frances Benjamin, 173, 190
Juliana (queen), 154

K

Kellogg, Miner K., **164**
Kemble, Fanny, **155**
Kennedy, Jacqueline
    Blue Room and, 83
    Diplomatic Reception Room and, 134
    Green Room and, 66, 73

    Library and, 114
    photographs, **1**, **56**
    portrait of, 120
    President's Dining Room and, 184, 187
    Queens' Sitting Room, and, 156
    Red Room and, 91, 92
    restoration program, 1, 172, 180
    tea table and, 156
    The White House: An Historic Guide, **xii**, 1, 184
    Treaty Room and, 172
    Yellow Oval Room and, 180, 182
Kennedy, John F.
    Blue Room and, 80
    Center Hall and, 177
    China Room and, 124
    Fish Room and, 218
    Green Room and, 73
    Guide, **xii**
    lain in state, 63
    Library and, 116
    Morning on the Seine and, 188
    Nobel Prize dinner (1962), **99**
    photographs, 1, **56**
    Queens' Sitting Room and, 156
    Red Room and, 91
    Resolute Desk, 206
    State Dining Room and, 99
    tea table, and, 156
    Treaty Room and, 172
King, Charles Bird, 118
King, Martin Luther, Jr., **63**
King, William, 114
kitchen, 140, 142–43, **142–43**
Kitchen Garden, **26**
Knox, Simmi, **112**

L

Ladies' Drawing Room, 180
Lafayette, Marquis de, 20, 118
Lafayette Park, 6, 20, **20**, 178
landscaping, 10, 24, 26
    See also flowers and shrubs; gardens; trees
Lannuier, Charles-Honoré, 94
Latrobe, Benjamin Henry, **14**, 29, 80, 91
L'Enfant, Pierre Charles, 6–7
L'Enfant plan, 6–7
Lenox china, 129
Lewis, Meriwether, 20, 46, 61
Library, 114, **114–19**, 116–18
light fixtures

Blue Room, 84
Cabinet Room, 164
East Room, 58, 60, **63**
Family Dining Room, **104**
Library, **116**
Oval Office, **203**
See also specific fixtures
lighthouse clock, **118**
Limited Nuclear Test Ban Treaty, 172
Lincoln, Abraham
  Blue Room and, 80
  Family Dining Room and, 104
  final speech by, 22, 178
  Green Room and, 70
  lain in state, **61**, 63
  Lincoln Bed and, 186
  Lincoln Bedroom and, 158
  Marine Band and, 32, 178
  North Corridor and, 178
  photographs, **168**
  portraits of, 101, **101**
  Red Room and, 92–93
  Willie's funeral and, 70
Lincoln, Mary Todd
  furnishings selected by, 164
  illustrations, **61**
  Lincoln Bed and, 158, 162–63
  Prince of Wales Room and, 164, 186
  state service china, **129**
Lincoln, Robert Todd, 101
Lincoln, Willie, 70, 186
Lincoln Bed, 70, 158, **158–60**, 162–63, 186
Lincoln Bedroom, 158, **158–61**, 162–64, **163**, 166
Lincoln Sitting Room, 158, 166, **166–67**, 168–69, 170
Longworth, Alice Roosevelt, 62, 148, 186
Louis XVI (style), 180
Louisiana Purchase, 20
Louisiana Territory, 46

M

Madison, Dolley
  Blue Room and, 80
  desserts and, 143
  fire (1814) and, 61, 64
  Ladies' Drawing Room and, 180
  portrait of, **95**
  purchases by, 128
  Red Room and, 91
  state service china, 129
  Washington's portrait and, 64

Madison, James, 52, 70, 80, 91
magnolias, 24
main entrance, 18, **18**
Maine, USS, 168
mantelpieces
  in China Room, 124
  in East Room, 60
  in Family Dining Room, 102
  in Green Room, 66, 72
  Library, **116**
  in Lincoln Sitting Room, 166
  marble, 66, 72
  in Oval Office, 198
  in Red Room, 72, 90
  in State Dining Room, 98, **99**
Map Room, 136, **136–38**, 138
maps, war, 138, **139**, 168
marble, 42, 52, 66, 72
Marine Band
  arrival ceremonies and, 46, 56
  Entrance Hall and, 47
  foreign heads of state and, 32–33
  Thomas Jefferson and, 47
  Abraham Lincoln and, 32, 178
  photographs, **48**
  as "The President's Own," 48
McKim, Charles Follen, 29
McKim, Mead & White, 29, 52, 100
McKinley, Ida Saxton, 176, 186
McKinley, William
  death, 169, 222
  dinner party by, **52**
  lain in state, 63
  Lincoln Sitting Room and, 168–69
  map room created by, 138
  office space of, 196
  President's Dining Room and, 186
  Press Room and, 222
  Treaty Room and, 172
  Yellow Oval Room and, 182
Millie (dog), **112**
Minerva clock, **49**, 122
Miranda, Francisco de, 70
mirrors, 62, 96, **100**, **101**, 122, 152
Monchousia (White Plume), **119**
Monet, Claude, 188
Monroe, James
  Blue Room and, 76, 80, 83, 84
  cruet stand sold by, **128**
  furniture purchased for, 84
  Green Room and, 70
  Indian delegation and, 118
  north grounds and, 10
  objects brought by, 122
  Pennsylvania Avenue and, 20

  portrait of, **80**
  receptions held by, 34
  redecorations by, 70, 76
  South Portico and, 31
  State Dining Room centerpiece and, 100
  state service china, 124, 130
  Treaty Room and, 172
Monroe Doctrine, 172
Montgomery, Benjamin F., 168, **169**
Montgomery, Robert, 138
Morning on the Seine (Monet painting), 188
Mountain at Bear Lake—Taos (O'Keeffe painting), **118**
movie theater, 227

N

National Geographic Society, 1
National Park Service, 6
National Society of Interior Designers, 132
Native Americans, 62, **62**, 118, **119**
neoclassical, 102, **128**, 156, 180
New Executive Office Building, 197
New Year's Day, 34, 80
Nicolay, George, 154, 162, 168, **168**
Nixon, Patricia, 120, **122**
Nixon, Richard M.
  Blue Room and, 82
  kitchen and, 143
  Lincoln Sitting Room and, 169
  Map Room and, 138
  office space of, 203
  Press Room and, 220, 222, 223
  Red Room and, 91
  Roosevelt Room and, 216, 218
  South Portico departure by, 22
  taping equipment and, 202
  West Wing and, 39
Nobel Prize dinner (1962), **99**
North Corridor, 178, **178–79**
North Door, 20, 22, **22**, 46, 82, 178
North Drive, **12**
north entrance, 148
north grounds, 8–13, **10–13**
North Portico, **14**, 22, 23, 34
North View, 14–23
Northwest Gate, **12**, **21**

O

oaths of office, 62, 63
Obama, Barack, **57**
Obama, Michelle, **57**
Odiot, Jean Baptiste-Claude, 122
Ohio buckeyes (trees), 10
O'Keeffe, Georgia, 118
Olmsted, Frederick Law, Jr., 26
Oval Office
    architecture, 202–5
    ceiling, 198
    construction, 39
    description, 198
    furnishings and decor, 198, **199–200**, **203**, 206, **206–7**
    history, 202–5
    photographs, **198–201**, **203**
    presidents and, 29, 39, 196, 198, 202, 203–4, **204**
    redecorations, 202–3
    shape of, 202
    uses, 197, 202, 203
oval rooms. *See* Blue Room; Diplomatic Reception Room; Oval Office; Yellow Oval Room

P

Paine, Thomas, 70
paintings
    Avenue in the Rain, The (Hassam), 206, **207**
    of Blue Room, **82**
    in Center Hall, 177
    in East Sitting Hall, 150, **151**
    in Green Room, 74
    Independence Hall in Philadelphia (Richardt), **75**
    In the White Mountains, New Hampshire (Sonntag), **151**
    in Library, 118–19
    in Lincoln Bedroom, **164**, **165**
    Morning on the Seine (Monet), 188
    Mountain at Bear Lake—Taos (O'Keeffe), **118**
    in Reception Room, 212
    in Red Room, **95**
    Rocky Mountain Landscape (Bierstadt), **95**
    Sailing Off the Coast (Heade), 151
    Sand Dunes at Sunset, Atlantic City (Tanner), **75**
    Watch Meeting - Dec. 31st 1862 - Waiting for the Hour (Carlton), **164**
    See also first ladies, portraits of; portraits; portraits, presidential
paneling, **63**, 96, 98, 126, 136
Payne, Melvin, **xii**
Peale, Rembrandt, 84
Pearce, Lorraine, **xii**
Pennsylvania Avenue, 20, **20**, **21**, 178
Peterson House, 170
pets, **112**
Phyfe, Duncan, 74, 114, 118
piano (Margaret Truman's), 186
Pierce, Franklin, 29, 90, 178
Pike, Zebulon, 46
Plains Indians, **62**
plateau (centerpiece), 96, **100**, 122
Platt, Emily, 61
platter, game ("Wild Turkey"), **126**
Polk, James K., 86, 128, 148, 164
Polk, Sarah, 128
porticos, 17, 31, 212
    See also North Portico; South Portico
portraits
    in China Room, 124
    of Emily Donelson, **154**
    in Family Dining Room, **102**
    of first ladies (*see* first ladies, portraits of)
    in Ground Floor Corridor, 108, 111, 112
    of Indians, 118, **119**
    of Fanny Kemble, **155**
    of Marquis de Lafayette, 118
    in Library, 118, **119**
    of presidents (*see* portraits, presidential)
    in Queens' Bedroom, **154**, **155**
    in Red Room, 90, 94, **95**, 112
    in Vermeil Room, **122**
portraits, presidential
    in Cabinet Room, 208
    in Cross Hall, 50, 52
    in East Room, 58, 60–61, 90
    in Entrance Hall, 49
    in Green Room, 66, **73**
    of Andrew Jackson, 154, **165**
    of Thomas Jefferson, **84**
    of Abraham Lincoln, 101, **101**
    of James Monroe, **80**
    in Red Room, 94
    of Franklin D. Roosevelt, 216, 218
    in Roosevelt Room, 216, 218
    of Theodore Roosevelt, 58, 64, **64**, 216, 218
    in State Dining Room, **101**
    of George Washington, 60–61, 64, **65**, 90
    See also busts
Powers, Hiram, 86, 90
Prairie Wolf (Shaumonekusse), **119**
Presidential Seal, 42, 129
President's Dining Room, 184–87, **184–87**
President's Park, 4, **4–5**, 6–7
President's Room, 196, 202, 210
"The President's Own" (Marine Band), 48
Press Area, **12**
Press Room, 220–23, **220–21**, **223**
Prince of Wales Room, 164, 186
prints, **164**
Public Papers of the Presidents, 212

Q

Queens' Bedroom, 152, **152–53**, 154
Queens' Sitting Room, 156, **156–57**

R

Reagan, Nancy, **113**
Reagan, Ronald, 191, 203, **223**
rebuilding, 34, 80, 120
Reception Room, 212–15, **212–14**
receptions
    Blue Room, 76, **81**
    East Room, 60, **60**
    New Year's, 34, 80
    Red Room, 72, 86, **86–92**, 90–94, 112
red salvia, 10, 81
Regency (style), 198
Remington, Frederic, 206
renovation (1902), 29
    Cross Hall, 50, 52
    Diplomatic Reception Room, 130, 132
    East Room, 63
    East Wing, 226
    Entrance Hall, 56
    Family Dining Room, 102, 105
    Grand Staircase, 52, 56, 190
    groin vaulting and, 110
    Ground Floor Corridor, 110, 111
    kitchen, 142, 143
    Lincoln Bedroom, 158
    piano and, 186
    Queens' Bedroom, 154
    Third Floor, 177
    time capsule and, 42
renovation (1948–52), 29

Diplomatic Reception Room, 132
East Sitting Hall, 148
Entrance Hall, 56
groin vaulting and, 110
kitchen, 143
Library bookcases and, 116
Map Room, 136
paneling and, 126, 136
State Dining Room, 96
time capsule and, 42
Vermeil Room, 120
repainting (1980), **16**, 39
Resolute desk, **183**, 198, **199**, **206**
restoration (after 1814 fire), 16, 29
restoration program (Jacqueline
    Kennedy's), 1, 172, 180
Richardt, Ferdinand, 75
Ritchie, Alexander, 164
Rockwell, Norman, 214
Rocky Mountain Landscape (Bierstadt
    painting), **95**
roof, 39
Roosevelt, Alice (later Longworth), 62,
    148, 186
Roosevelt, Edith, 102, **102**, 112, 127,
    176
Roosevelt, Eleanor, 93, **122**, 143
Roosevelt, Franklin D.
    Cabinet Room and, 210
    death and funeral, **23**, 63, 211
    East Sitting Hall and, 148
    East Wing and, 224, 226
    fireside chats, 132, **133**
    formal gardens and, 26
    inauguration (1945), 32, **32**
    kitchen and, 143
    Library and, 116
    Lincoln portrait and, 101
    Map Room and, 136, 138
    Oval Office and, 39, 202
    portrait of, 216, 218
    presidential coat of arms and, 206
    Resolute desk, 206
    Roosevelt Room and, 216, 218
    State Dining Room and, 98, 99
    swimming pool and, 222, **222**
    war maps and, 138, 139
    West Wing and, 39, 196–97
    Yellow Oval Room and, 182
Roosevelt, Theodore
    awards and honors, 216
    Blue Room and, 80, 82
    Cabinet Room and, **210**
    Conservation Conference and, 62
    East Room and, 60
    Family Dining Room and, 104, 105

Lincoln Bedroom and, 163
office space of, 196, 202
portrait of, 58, 64, **64**, 216, 218
Resolute desk, 206
Roosevelt Room and, 216
State Dining Room and, 96, 98, 99
state service china and, 124
West Wing and, 196, 202
See also renovation (1902)
Roosevelt renovation. *See* renovation
    (1902)
Roosevelt Room, 216–19, **216–17**
Rose Bedroom, 152
Rose Garden, **13**, 26, **27**, 33, 197, **205**
rugs and carpeting
    Blue Room, 76
    Cabinet Room, 208
    Diplomatic Reception Room, 130
    Family Dining Room, 102
    Green Room, 76
    Library, **116**
    Lincoln Sitting Room, 166
    Oval Office, 198, **199–200**
    Queens' Bedroom, 152
Rundell, Philip, 122

S

Sadat, Anwar al-, 62
Sailing Off the Coast (Heade painting),
    151
Sand Dunes at Sunset, Atlantic City
    (Tanner painting), **75**
sandstone, 16
sanitary fairs, 162
Sargent, John Singer, 64
Schurz, Carl, **183**
screen, Tiffany, 46, **47**, 52
sculpture (Remington), **206**
    See also busts
Second Floor, 8, 54, 102, 197
    See also specific rooms
Secret Service, 214, 226
senators, 202
Seymour, John and Thomas, 150
Sharitarish (Wicked Chief), **119**
Shaumonekusse (Prairie Wolf), **119**
Shaw, John, 134
Shikler, Aaron, 112
shrubs and flowers, 6, 10, 24, 81
silver, 120, 122, **123**
Simon Willard and Son, **118**
Situation Room, 194
sofas, 76, 80, **94**, 212

Sofia (queen), 154
Sonntag, William, 151
Sonya (queen), 154
south grounds, 24, **24–25**
South Lawn, **26**, 32–33
South Portico
    archway, 32
    balcony, 31, 39, 183
    construction, 31, 34
    photographs, **31**, **32**
    presidents and, 22, 31, 32, **32**, 39
    uses, 32
South View, 26–29
Spanish-American War, 138, 168, 172
spittoons, 148, **172**
stars, brass, 42
State and official Dinners, **57**, 98–99
State Dining Room
    architecture, 98–99
    description, 96
    doors, **53**, **105**
    Family Dining Room and, 105
    fireplace, **99**
    first ladies and, 99
    furnishings and decor, 96, 99, 100,
        100, **101**, 122
    heating in, 91
    history, 98–99
    paneling in, 96, 98
    photographs, **96–97**, **98**, **100–101**
    presidential portraits in, 101, **101**
    presidents and, 96, 98, 99, 100, 102,
        104
    renovation, 98
    uses, 98–99
State Floor, 8, 17, 108
    See also specific rooms
state parlors. *See* Blue Room; Green
    Room; Red Room
State Rooms. *See* Blue Room; East
    Room; Green Room; Red Room;
    State Dining Room
state service china. *See* china, state
    service
Stellwagen, C. K., 163
Stone, Harlan Fiske, **211**
stone balustrade, 15, **15**
stone shell, 39
stonework, 16–18
Storr, Paul, 122
Stuart, Gilbert, 60, 61, 64, 94, 95
Sully, Thomas, 155
swimming pools, **27**, 29, 222, **222**, 223

T

tables
  cabinet table, 170, 208, **208–9**
  Family Dining Room, **219**
  Fish Room, **219**
  gilded pier table, **49**
  gueridons, **94**
  mahogany center table, **146–47**
  mahogany console tables, **101**
  mahogany work table, **74**
  rosewood center table, **164**
  State Dining Room, 99, **101**
  tea table, 156, **157**
  Vermeil Room, 120
Taft, William Howard, 29, 39, 142,
  196, 198, 202, **204**
Tanner, Henry Ossawa, 75
taping equipment, 202
Taylor, Zachary, 63
telegraphs, 168
telephones, 168
Temporary Office, 196
tennis court, **26**
theater, movie, 227
Third Floor, 8, 15, 39, 177
Thomas Jefferson Memorial, 7, 82
Tiffany, Louis Comfort, 46, 47, 81, 91
Tiffany screen, 46, **47**, 52
Tiffany silver, 122
time capsules, 42, 52
treaties, 172
Treaty of Paris, 172
Treaty on the Limitation of Antiballis-
  tic Missile Systems, 172
Treaty Room, 170, **170–73**, 172
trees, 6, 10, 24, 26
Truman, Bess, **56**, **211**
Truman, Harry S.
  Cross Hall and, 52
  East Room and, 60
  Family Dining Room and, 102
  Fish Room and, 218
  Grand Staircase and, 56
  Lincoln Bedroom and, 162, 163
  north grounds and, 10
  photographs, **56**, **211**
  presidential coat of arms and, 198
  State Dining Room and, 102
  Truman Balcony, 29, 31, 39, 183
  Yellow Oval Room and, 183
  See also renovation (1948–52)
Truman, Margaret (later Daniels), **56**,
  186

Truman renovation. *See* renovation
  (1948–52)
trumeau, 152
Tyler, Julia Gardiner, 111

U

United States Magazine, **90**
usher, chief, 48
Usher's Room, **48**

V

Van Buren, Abraham, 90
Van Buren, Angelica, 90
Van Buren, Martin, 46, 76, 80, 86, 90,
  164
Vanderlyn, John, 80
vegetable garden, 6
vermeil objects, 120, 122, **123**
Vermeil Room, 120, **120–23**, 122
Vespucci, Amerigo, 76
Victoria (queen), 206
"Views of North America" (wallpaper),
  135
Volk, Leonard, 112

W

wall coverings
  Blue Room, 76, 82
  Cabinet Room, 210
  Diplomatic Reception Room, **135**
  Green Room, 66
  Lincoln Bedroom, 163
  Lincoln Sitting Room, 166,
  Oval Office, **203**
  President's Dining Room, 184, 187
  Treaty Room, 170
  "Views of North America," **135**
Walter, Thomas U., 29
war maps, 138, **139**, 168
War of 1812, 34, 61
Washington, Booker T., 104
Washington, George
  Blue Room and, 80
  bust of, 112
  East Room and, 61
  portraits of, 60–61, 64, **65**, 90
  President's Park and, 6–7
  stonework and, 18
  White House design and, 24, 34
Washington, Martha, 61
Washington Monument, 7, **7**

*Watch Meeting – Dec. 31st 1862 – Wait-
  ing for the Hour* (Carlton painting),
  165
Waud, Alfred, 61
Webster, Daniel, 129
weddings, 62, **81**
Wedgwood, 238
West Colonnade, **13**, **27**, 33, **33**
West Sitting Hall, 188, **188–91**, 190–91
West Wing
  architects, 29
  architecture, 196–97
  construction, 34
  description, 194
  fire (1929), 39, 196
  history, 196–97
  illustrations, **13**, **27**, **215**
  original, 202
  photographs, **19**, **33**, **194–95**, **196**,
  197
  presidents and, 19, 34, 39, 196–97,
  202
  remodeling, 39
  uses, 194
White, Stanford, 101
White House
  architects, 29
  construction timeline, 34, 39
  design, 24, 34
  main central block, 30, **30**
  photographs and illustrations, **7**, **14**,
  35–38
  size, 8, 14, 24, 39
  two-hundredth anniversary, 129
White House collection, 80, 120, **123**
White House Mess, 194
White Plume (Monchousia), **119**
whitewash, **16**, 34
Wicked Chief (Sharitarish), **119**
"Wild Turkey" (game platter), **126**
Wilhelmina (queen), 154
Wilson, Edith, 127, 129
Wilson, Woodrow, 124, **129**, 202
window surrounds, 17, **17**, **18**
window treatments. *See* curtains
windows
  East Sitting Hall, 146, **147**
  fan windows, 146, **147**, 149, 191
  North Corridor, 178
  Red Room, **90**
  State Floor, **17**
  West Sitting Hall, 188, **188–89**
Winslow, Lorenzo S., 29, 52, 116, 132

Woman's Christian Temperance
    Union, 104
work table, mahogany (1810), **74**
World War II, 138, 139, 177
Wyeth, Henriette, 122
Wyeth, Nathan C., 29

Y

Yellow Oval Room, **180–83**, 182–83

Z

Zavala, Margarita, **57**